Essential Survival Projects for Off-Grid Living: The Ultimate No-Grid Preparedness Kit for Busy People

Master Your Self-Sufficiency in Moments of Crisis

Edward Snell

Essential Survival Projects for Off-Grid Living:
The Ultimate No-Grid Preparedness Kit for Busy People
Copyright © 2025 by Edward Snell

Paperback ISBN: 978-1-966283-21-8
Hardcover ISBN: 978-1-966283-22-5

1. Main category—Books › Sports & Outdoors › Outdoors & Nature › Hiking & Camping › Instructional
2. Other category—Books › Politics & Social Sciences › Social Sciences › Disaster Relief
3. Other category—Books › Crafts, Hobbies & Home › How-to & Home Improvements › Do-It-Yourself

Published by: AR PRESS
Roger L. Brooks, Publisher
roger@americanrealpublishing.com
americanrealpublishing.com

Table of Contents

Introduction

Imagine waking up one morning only to find the world as you know it has ceased to function. The lights don't come on, the water doesn't run, and your phone, your lifeline to the modern world, is nothing more than a brick. There's no electricity, no internet, and no immediate signs of help. You're in a gridless world where the infrastructure we depend on daily has vanished. *How would you survive? What would you eat? Where would you find water? How would you protect your loved ones?*

The notion of a postapocalyptic world can sound like the stuff of movies, but the potential for grid failure is very real. Natural disasters, cyberattacks, solar flares, or even large-scale political upheavals can trigger a collapse of the systems that keep our world running. In the aftermath, the conveniences of modern life would no longer be at our fingertips. Without electricity, transportation networks, or communication systems, society as we know it could fall into chaos. Now, more than ever, it's crucial to adopt a survival mindset, learning the skills necessary to adapt and thrive in an unpredictable, gridless future.

Survival isn't simply about knowing how to start a fire or hunt for food. It begins in the mind. Adaptability, resilience, and a calm demeanor are your most valuable assets in a gridless world. When you face a world without modern conveniences, your ability to adapt to rapidly changing circumstances is essential. Developing a survival mindset means being ready to handle uncertainty, stress, and even fear. It's about maintaining a psychological edge when everything around you is falling apart.

Welcome to *Essential Survival Projects for Off-Grid Living: The Ultimate No-Grid Preparedness Kit for Busy People. Master Your Self-Sufficiency in Moments of Crisis,* where you will learn the basics of everything necessary to survive in a gridless situation.

When disaster strikes, it's easy to panic. But panic leads to poor decision-making, which can be fatal in survival situations. Imagine being stranded without access to clean water. If you don't stay calm and approach the problem logically, perhaps by finding a river or collecting rainwater, you can make decisions out of desperation. In many survival stories, those who made it through didn't always have the most resources, but they had the mental toughness to endure. They adapted and found solutions.

The importance of mental resilience can't be overstated. Survivors in extreme conditions often talk about the power of mindset. Take the story of Aron Ralston, who famously survived a canyoneering accident by amputating his own arm after days of being trapped under a boulder. His physical strength was important, but his mental resolve ultimately saved his life (Serena, 2023). This kind of resilience is something we can all cultivate before a crisis strikes.

In a world without a functioning grid, knowing basic survival skills isn't optional; it's essential. The time to learn these skills is now, not when you're already in the middle of a crisis. By practicing and refining your abilities, you prepare yourself practically and build confidence. Confidence in your ability to survive can drastically improve your chances in a postapocalyptic scenario.

Let's start with some key skills:

- **Finding and purifying water:** Without access to clean water, most people wouldn't last beyond a few days. Knowing how to locate natural water sources, like rivers, lakes, or rainwater collection, is critical. But water alone isn't enough; you must purify it to avoid life-threatening bacteria and contaminants. Learning simple purification techniques like boiling water or using portable filters can keep you alive in a gridless world. In the next chapter, we will learn about this in detail.

- **Foraging and hunting for food:** The food supply chain would likely be one of the first things to collapse in a major crisis. Supermarkets would empty within days, and then what? Foraging for edible plants, trapping small animals, or fishing could become your primary sources of nourishment. Learning what's safe to eat in your local environment and practicing now can prevent you from making fatal mistakes later.

- **Building shelter and fire:** Exposure to the elements is one of the most immediate dangers in survival situations. You need to know how to construct makeshift shelters from natural materials to protect yourself from the cold, heat, or rain. Equally important is the ability to start a fire, which can keep you warm, allow you to cook, and provide a psychological boost in the dark, uncertain nights ahead.

These are just a few of the essential skills, but they represent the foundation of survival in a world where modern conveniences are no longer available. The more you practice and master these skills before any disaster occurs, the more empowered and self-sufficient you'll feel. That empowerment builds resilience, which can carry you through even the most dire situations.

While individual skills are required, survival in a postapocalyptic world is often a collective effort. The idea of the lone survivor, while appealing in books and movies, is far less practical in reality. In fact, history shows humans thrive when they come together, pool resources, and support one another. Think about how communities band together after natural disasters. People share food, water, and knowledge. They provide emotional and physical support to help each other through hard times.

In a gridless world, building or joining a network of people with diverse skills and resources could be the difference between life and death. Perhaps one person knows how to hunt, another can purify water, and someone else has medical knowledge. By working together, you can create a support system that enhances your chances of survival.

Forming alliances also helps distribute the mental load of surviving. The emotional toll of isolation in an apocalyptic scenario can be overwhelming. Humans are social creatures, and we thrive on connection. By sharing your struggles and successes with others, you maintain your psychological well-being, which is just as important as staying physically alive.

We may not know when—or if—a catastrophic event will knock out the grid. But what we do know is that by adopting a survival mindset, learning essential skills, and building strong networks of support, we can significantly improve our chances of thriving in a postapocalyptic world. Preparation is empowerment, and there's no better time to start building your resilience for the future.

Essential Survival Projects for Off-Grid Living isn't just a manual for navigating disaster—it's a guide to mastering the mindset, skills, and connections that will ensure your survival when the world as you know it ceases to exist.

So, are you ready to face this world?

Chapter 1:

Understanding the Gridless Landscape

Think of a world where the conveniences we take for granted—electricity, running water, and internet access—suddenly vanish. It's not a momentary blackout but a permanent shift in which the systems that power our lives collapse, and society begins to unravel.

In this chapter, we'll dive into what it means to live in a gridless world where modern infrastructure no longer exists and help you understand the scale of change such a transition would entail.

A gridless landscape is more than the absence of electricity; it's a fundamental shift in how we live, interact, and survive. To prepare for such a scenario, you first need to recognize the signs of grid failure. Often, these indicators are present long before the final collapse. Understanding them gives you a critical advantage, allowing you to act early and protect yourself and your loved ones.

Recognizing Signs of Grid Failure

The signs of an impending grid collapse are often subtle at first but can quickly escalate if you know what to look for. By paying attention to leading indicators like social unrest, supply chain disruptions, utility failures, and policy changes, you can spot the early warning signals and take action before it's too late.

Social Unrest

One of the first visible cracks in a failing grid is the breakdown of social order. Social unrest often starts as localized incidents—protests, riots, or civil disobedience triggered by political instability, economic inequality, or resource shortages. These events can quickly spiral out of control, leading to widespread violence and lawlessness.

For example, during the 2020 COVID-19 pandemic, many cities around the world experienced waves of protests and unrest. In some cases, the stress on government systems led to delayed emergency responses and strained law enforcement. While these events didn't lead to total societal collapse, they offered a glimpse of what happens when social order breaks down.

In a gridless scenario, social unrest can escalate even further. Envision mass panic as essential services, like banking or healthcare, go offline indefinitely. The result is chaos: looting, violence, and a general breakdown of law and order. If you start noticing heightened tensions in your community or nationwide protests over resource scarcity, it may be time to start planning for grid failure.

Supply Chain Disruptions

A grid collapse often begins with disruptions to the supply chain. The global supply chain is an intricate system that relies heavily on communication networks, transportation infrastructure, and stable production facilities. When these systems fail, the flow of goods, especially essentials like food, fuel, and medicine, comes to a halt.

Consider how quickly store shelves emptied during natural disasters like Hurricane Katrina in 2005 (Palin, 2017). Panic buying left grocery stores barren within hours, and it took weeks for supply lines to recover. Now, imagine a situation where these disruptions are permanent. Without the internet, transportation networks, or fuel, grocery stores wouldn't restock, pharmacies would run out of medicine, and fuel stations would shut down indefinitely.

The early signs of a supply chain collapse often manifest as delayed shipments, rising prices, and product shortages. If you begin to notice certain items, especially essentials, are becoming harder to find or are skyrocketing in price, this is a red flag for more extensive disruptions ahead. The collective effect of a strained supply chain will soon be felt across industries, leading to widespread shortages that could hasten the collapse of society.

Utility Failures

Utilities, like electricity, water, and gas, are the backbone of modern life. When these fail, society quickly unravels. One of the most apparent signs that the grid is beginning to collapse is widespread utility outages that aren't quickly fixed.

These failures can stem from a variety of causes, including cyberattacks, extreme weather, or even aging infrastructure.

Take the 2021 Texas power grid failure as an example. Millions of people were left without heat and electricity for days during an unprecedented winter storm (Buchele, 2023). While this was a temporary failure, it highlighted just how fragile our utility systems can be. In a prolonged grid-down scenario, these failures would be permanent, with no crews available to restore power, fix water lines, or ensure gas distribution.

The early signs of utility failures often include rolling blackouts, water shortages, or intermittent service disruptions. If these outages become more frequent and lengthy, it may indicate the grid is failing. In such cases, you must be prepared to find alternative sources of power, water, and heat to survive.

Policy Changes

Government policies can be both a cause and a consequence of grid failure. In the early stages of societal collapse, governments often try to maintain control by enacting sweeping policy changes that may restrict individual freedoms or impose new restrictions on resource use. These policies can include rationing food, controlling fuel distribution, or implementing martial law.

The early signs of policy-driven grid collapse include sudden changes in laws related to resource management, increasing government surveillance, and more frequent emergency declarations. If you notice governments beginning to implement strict rationing policies or curfews, it's a signal that resources are running thin and the infrastructure supporting modern life is faltering.

Preparing for a Gridless Future

Now that you understand the signs of grid failure, social unrest, supply chain disruptions, utility failures, and policy changes, you can take the necessary steps to prepare. It's not about waiting for the worst to happen; it's about staying vigilant and ready to act when the first cracks appear.

When you spot these warning signs, staying calm and enacting your survival plan is key. Stock up on essentials, like food, water, and medical supplies, before shortages become critical. Develop your skills in self-sufficiency, from learning how to purify water to growing your own food. Most importantly, start forming a network of people you can rely on in times of crisis. Survival in a gridless world is much easier when you share resources and knowledge with others.

Living in a gridless landscape will require a radical shift in how we view and navigate the world. It's not just about losing electricity. It's also about adapting to an entirely new way of life. Recognizing the early signs of grid failure can give you the precious time needed to prepare and respond effectively. The more you understand the depth of change a grid collapse would bring, the better positioned you'll be to thrive in a future where modern conveniences are a distant memory.

Evaluating the Impact on Daily Life

When the grid collapses, the most immediate and over-whelming challenge will be adjusting to the disruption of our daily routines. From the way we gather information to how we move from place to place and access basic resources, the shift will be nothing short of life-altering. This section will explore how life would change in a gridless world, examining the disruption of routine, the loss of access to information, mobility challenges, and the availability of essential resources.

Disruption of Routine

Our daily routines are deeply intertwined with the conveniences provided by modern infrastructure. The grid powers nearly everything we do, from the moment we wake up to the sound of an electric alarm clock to the coffee we brew, the transportation we take to work, and the devices we use to communicate. When the grid fails, these routines are the first casualties.

For example, consider something as simple as your morning routine. Without electricity, your alarm clock won't go off. If you rely on a phone or smart device to wake you up, it won't work either if the battery has died and there's no power to recharge it. What about your coffee maker, fridge, and stove?

Useless. Suddenly, you're starting your day in the dark, both literally and metaphorically.

Beyond the small inconveniences, larger disruptions soon follow. If you work in an office, school, or another facility dependent on electricity, those places will close. Schools may shutter indefinitely, grocery stores will empty out, and even communication networks will go silent. Without power, refrigeration fails, meaning food spoilage becomes a major issue within days. Water systems may also break down, leaving homes without running water. This forces you to shift to survival mode, turning basic tasks into time-consuming challenges that require planning and effort.

Access to Information

One of the most profound changes in a gridless world will be the loss of instant access to information. Right now, we live in a hyper-connected world where information is just a few clicks away. Whether it's the latest news, weather updates, or advice on how to fix a leaking pipe, you can find nearly anything online in seconds. In a world without power and the internet, this changes overnight.

Without the internet, how will you stay informed about what's happening in the wider world? The news that typically reaches you through your phone, television, or computer will no longer be available. You'll have to rely on alternative methods of communication and information-gathering, such as shortwave radios, in-person updates, or even bulletin boards if they still exist.

During the 2003 blackout in the Northeastern United States and parts of Canada, which affected more than fifty million people, residents found themselves suddenly cut off from real-time updates. Without electricity, people turned to battery-powered radios for news and neighbors shared information face-to-face (History.com Editors, 2018). This event lasted just a few days but offered a picture of how we'll need to adapt in a prolonged gridless scenario. Accessing accurate information will require creativity and resourcefulness—two qualities critical for survival.

The ability to communicate with others is another aspect of information access that will be severely limited. Cell phones and landlines will quickly become unreliable, if not useless, without the power to charge them or maintain networks. You'll need to have alternative ways to reach out to friends, family, or communities, whether through walkie-talkies, ham radios, or other low-tech solutions.

Mobility Challenges

Getting from point A to point B is another part of daily life that we take for granted, yet it's heavily reliant on the grid. Without functioning gas stations, traffic lights, and public transportation systems, mobility will be severely restricted in a gridless world. This will have a lasting impact on your ability to move around and how you obtain resources, connect with others, and stay safe.

We all know how modern transportation relies on both fuel and technology. Cars need gasoline, and gas stations depend on electricity to pump fuel. In the absence of power, refueling becomes a significant challenge. Even if you have a full tank, your driving ability may still be limited by road conditions, which could become unsafe owing to a lack of functioning traffic signals, accidents, or roadblocks.

Public transportation systems, including trains, buses, and subways, will also grind to a halt, leaving many people stranded or isolated. In urban areas, the loss of public transportation can lead to overcrowding and a scramble for resources as people try to leave the city. On the other hand, rural areas may see a less immediate impact on mobility but will suffer as supply routes are cut off, making it challenging to bring essentials like food and medicine.

Walking and biking may become the primary means of transportation in many places. While this can seem like a manageable adjustment, it's important to remember mobility challenges can limit your access to crucial resources, especially if you live far from supply hubs or safe zones. Travel becomes not just about getting from one place to another but ensuring you have the means to do so safely and efficiently.

Resource Availability

Of all the challenges posed by a gridless world, the scarcity of resources is perhaps the most pressing. Modern supply chains are incredibly complex and operate on tight schedules, with goods often arriving just in time to meet demand. When the grid goes down, this delicate balance is immediately disrupted, and the availability of food, water, fuel, and medical supplies becomes a central concern.

One of the first resources to become scarce is clean drinking water. Municipal water systems depend on electricity to pump and purify water, meaning a grid collapse can leave entire cities without access to clean water. This was evident in Puerto Rico after Hurricane Katrina in 2005, when the island's water system was crippled, leading to widespread shortages and outbreaks of waterborne diseases (Palin, 2017). In a prolonged grid-down scenario, you'll need alternative water sources or ways to purify it, such as water filters, rain collection systems, or purification tablets.

Food shortages will also become a critical issue. Without refrigeration, food spoils quickly. Supply chain disruptions will halt the regular restocking of grocery stores, and shelves will be bare within days. It's crucial to think about long-term food security by growing your own food, preserving nonperishable items, or having a well-thought-out stockpile.

As mentioned earlier, fuel will also be in short supply, impacting transportation, heating, and cooking. Many people rely on natural gas or electricity to heat their homes and prepare meals. In a gridless world, alternative energy sources like solar power, firewood, or propane will become essential for survival.

Lastly, medical resources will be short, which poses a serious threat to people with chronic conditions or those who require regular medical care. Pharmacies will run out of medication, and hospitals, without power, will be unable to function properly. Having a well-stocked first-aid kit and knowledge of basic medical care will be imperative. In the longer term, learning how to use herbal remedies or homeopathic treatments could be lifesaving, as these might be the only available options for many health issues.

Adapting Mindset for Change

In a postapocalyptic world where the comforts and conveniences of modern life no longer exist, survival depends on practical skills and the mindset you adopt. The ability to embrace change, adapt quickly, and maintain mental resilience will make all the difference. This section focuses on the psychological aspect of survival and how to develop the right mindset for facing an unpredictable, gridless future.

Embracing Uncertainty

In a world without a grid, uncertainty will become the norm. The routines and stability most people are accustomed to (knowing where the next meal is coming from, having access to information at all times, or enjoying a reliable power supply) will no longer exist. This type of uncertainty can be deeply unsettling, but learning to embrace it is its remedy.

One of the first steps in embracing uncertainty is accepting that you cannot control everything. This is where mindset becomes powerful. If you're constantly struggling to impose old patterns of predictability on an unpredictable environment, you'll quickly burn out. Therefore, it's essential to develop a sense of flexibility. Expect things to go wrong. Prepare for setbacks and have multiple contingency plans in place. When you let go of the need for control and instead focus on adapting, you'll be better equipped to navigate the challenges that come your way.

A real-world example of this can be seen in survivors of natural disasters, such as Hurricane Maria in 2005. Many who survived the storm's aftermath did so not just because they had resources but because they accepted the situation was chaotic and acted accordingly. They embraced flexibility—moving to new shelters when needed, improvising with available resources, and accepting that their previous lives were indefinitely on hold.

Developing Problem-Solving Skills

Survival in a gridless world will require more than physical endurance; it will demand the ability to solve problems on the fly. Without modern conveniences, many of the problems you face will be new and unpredictable, from finding clean drinking water to repairing a vital tool without the proper parts.

The key to developing effective problem-solving skills is to think creatively and resourcefully. You need to begin by practicing problem-solving in everyday life. For example, if you encounter a minor household issue, like a leaky faucet or a broken appliance, try to solve it without immediately relying on YouTube or professional help. This kind of hands-on, trial-and-error approach will build confidence and ingenuity.

In a gridless world, you'll often need to solve problems with limited resources. MacGyver-style thinking, using common items in unconventional ways, will become essential. A piece of string can serve as a fishing line, or an empty bottle can be used to purify water. Developing this kind of creative problem-solving ability starts now by looking at everyday objects through a survival lens. What can you repurpose if you can no longer access stores or supplies?

Take inspiration from those who have lived in extreme conditions. For instance, during the Siege of Sarajevo in the 1990s, people found incredibly inventive ways to solve fundamental problems. With utilities cut off, residents used everything from discarded plastic to old car batteries to create makeshift stoves, water filters, and generators (Maček, 2017). Thinking outside the box and making do with what's available can turn dire situations into manageable ones.

Fostering a Growth Mindset

A growth mindset is the belief that abilities and intelligence can be developed through effort, learning, and perseverance. In contrast, a fixed mindset assumes our abilities are set in stone and cannot be improved. In a survival situation, fostering a growth mindset can greatly increase your chances of thriving in an unpredictable world.

Why is this important?

In a gridless setting, you'll be confronted with many new challenges you've never encountered before. Those with a fixed mindset may believe they lack the necessary skills or abilities to overcome these challenges and, as a result, may give up quickly. On the other hand, people with a growth mindset will see each obstacle as an opportunity to learn something new or to become more resourceful.

For example, let's say your first attempt at building a fire fails. A person with a fixed mindset might think, "I'm just not good at this," and quit. Someone with a growth mindset will reflect on what went wrong, learn from it, and try again, adjusting their technique. Over time, these small successes build into larger competencies, transforming you into a more capable and confident survivor.

One practical way to foster a growth mindset is to continually challenge yourself with new skills. Whether it's learning how to grow your own food, practicing first aid, or mastering navigation without GPS, these skills prepare you for a potential crisis and cultivate an attitude of learning and growth. Every new skill you learn becomes a resource you can draw on when survival is at stake.

Building Emotional Resilience

Emotional resilience is the skill of adapting to stressful situations and bouncing back from adversity. Maintaining emotional resilience will be just as important as physical survival skills in a world without the grid. The stress of constant uncertainty, scarcity of resources, and potential isolation can wear down even the strongest people, making it necessary to develop strategies for managing emotions and maintaining mental health.

One key to building emotional resilience is focusing on what you can control. This involves shifting your mindset from worrying about the future to concentrating on the present moment. Practicing mindfulness techniques, such as meditation, deep breathing exercises, or simply being aware of your surroundings, can help you manage stress and anxiety in a chaotic environment. In fact, studies have shown mindfulness can improve emotional regulation and reduce feelings of distress, making it an important tool for any survivalist (Guendelman et al., 2017).

Another aspect of emotional resilience is building a support network, even in a gridless world. Survival is not a solitary pursuit. Having trusted people you can rely on for emotional support and shared problem-solving can provide a sense of stability in unstable times. Building strong relationships within your survival group, or even maintaining connections with nearby neighbors, can create a sense of community. This emotional backing can be a lifeline, especially when faced with difficult decisions or long periods of uncertainty.

Identifying Immediate Needs

Whether faced with a natural disaster, societal collapse, or any other crisis that disrupts modern conveniences, your immediate needs will dictate your actions. Understanding how to identify these needs and plan accordingly is essential for anyone seeking to thrive in uncertain times.

Let's break down the basic survival priorities, assess personal resources and plans for sustainability, and emphasize the importance of emergency preparedness planning.

Basic Survival Priorities

When considering survival in gridless circumstances, it's paramount to understand the hierarchy of basic needs. Drawing inspiration from Maslow's hierarchy, we can outline the essentials that must be addressed first (Cherry, 2024). Let's have a look at them:

- **Water:** The most immediate concern in any survival scenario is access to clean water. Humans can survive without food for weeks, but survival is measured in days without water. Knowing how to find, purify, and store water should be at the top of your list. For instance, collecting rainwater or using a portable water filter can ensure you have safe drinking water.

- **Food:** Next comes food. In a survival situation, the priority shifts from a diverse diet to caloric intake.

Learning to identify edible plants and to hunt, fish, or trap animals can give essential nutrients. For example, dandelions are not just weeds; they're nutritious and can be used in salads or teas.

- **Shelter:** Protecting yourself from the elements is required for maintaining health and well-being. Your shelter should provide insulation, safety from predators, and a way to store supplies. A simple tarp can serve as a temporary shelter, but understanding how to build a more permanent structure using natural materials can provide long-term security.

- **Fire:** Fire promotes warmth, cooking, and protection. It can also serve as a signal for help. Knowing how to start a fire without modern conveniences, such as using flint and steel or friction methods, is a key skill.

- **Security:** In chaotic environments, personal safety becomes paramount. Establishing a secure area where you can rest and feel safe is vital. This could mean fortifying your shelter or creating a perimeter to deter unwanted visitors.

Addressing these primary survival priorities helps establish a solid foundation for your immediate needs. Think of this as your survival checklist. Ensuring each item is accounted for will give you the best chance of thriving in a challenging environment.

Assessing Personal Resources

Once you've identified your basic survival priorities, it's time to take stock of the resources at your disposal. This includes not only physical supplies but also skills and knowledge.

- **Inventory of supplies:** Begin by inventorying what you have on hand. Look for nonperishable food items, water storage containers, first-aid supplies, and tools. For example, canned goods, rice, and pasta are great long-term food supplies. If you have a camping stove or portable cooking equipment, that's a significant advantage.

- **Personal skills:** Evaluate your skills and how they can contribute to survival. Are you a good cook? Do you have gardening experience? Can you navigate using a map and compass? Skills in sewing, woodworking, or even basic mechanical repair can prove invaluable in a crisis.

- **Network of support:** Your relationships can be a vital resource. Consider your family, friends, and community. Who has skills or resources that could be helpful? For example, a neighbor with gardening expertise can assist in growing food, while a friend with medical training can help manage health issues.

Understanding your personal resources is the first step to making informed decisions during a crisis. When you know what you have to work with, you can better plan how to address your immediate needs and what gaps you need to fill.

Planning for Sustainability

Sustainability is a crucial aspect of survival in a gridless future. It's not enough to simply meet your immediate needs; you must also consider how to sustain yourself and your loved ones over the long term.

- **Food production:** One of the most effective ways to ensure ongoing food security is by cultivating your own food. Start a garden with easy-to-grow crops like tomatoes, potatoes, and leafy greens. Even if space is limited, container gardening can be a viable option. Additionally, consider learning about permaculture principles, which focus on creating sustainable agricultural ecosystems.

- **Water conservation:** Setting a reliable water source is crucial for sustainability. Explore methods for rainwater harvesting or setting up a gray water recycling system. Understanding how to purify water from natural sources can ensure ongoing access to clean water.

- **Energy solutions:** Finding alternative energy sources becomes a priority without the grid. Consider investing in solar panels, wind turbines, or even learning to harness energy through small-scale hydroelectric systems if you have access to running water. Even simple solutions, like using a solar oven to cook food, can help reduce dependence on traditional energy sources.

- **Building community:** Sustainability extends beyond individual efforts. Building a community of like-minded people can create a network of support and resource sharing. Consider forming groups focused on skills exchange, where members can teach each other essential skills, from gardening to carpentry.

Long-term planning for sustainability will give peace of mind and the ability to thrive even when immediate resources run low. The more you can create a self-sustaining environment, the more resilient you will be to challenges that arise.

Emergency Preparedness Planning

No one wants to think about a crisis, but preparation is vital to minimizing its impact. Emergency preparedness planning allows you to respond effectively when disaster strikes. Here are some key components to include in your plan:

- **Emergency kit:** Assemble a comprehensive emergency kit that includes basic supplies. This should contain food, water, first-aid supplies, tools, and personal hygiene items. A good rule of thumb is to prepare for at least seventy-two hours of self-sufficiency.

- **Communication plan:** In an emergency, knowing how to communicate with family or friends can be helpful. Establish a plan for how to contact each other, especially if mobile networks are down. Consider creating a meet-up location where everyone can gather if communication fails.

- **Practice drills:** Just as fire drills prepare you for emergencies, practicing your survival skills and emergency plans can enhance your readiness. Conduct drills to test your emergency responses, such as setting up your emergency shelter or utilizing your emergency kit.

- **Stay informed:** Keep informed about potential threats in your area, whether they are natural disasters, political unrest, or other crises. Sign up for local emergency alerts and monitor news sources. Being aware of your surroundings will help you react quickly and effectively when needed.

Emergency preparedness is not a one-time task but a continuous process. Regularly review and update your emergency plan to ensure it remains relevant to your circumstances.

By establishing a solid foundation of survival knowledge and practical skills, you equip yourself to navigate the complexities of a postapocalyptic world. Remember, survival is not just about the tools you have; it's about the mindset you cultivate and the connections you forge with others. Embrace the journey of preparedness and self-sufficiency, and you'll find yourself better equipped to face whatever challenges come your way.

Chapter 2:

Developing Essential Survival Skills

When the grid goes down, immediate access to medical care can become limited or even impossible. In these moments, you need to know how to manage injuries and perform basic first aid, as it will make the difference between life and death.

This chapter explores essential first-aid techniques to ensure you're equipped to handle common injuries and medical emergencies in a survival scenario. Understanding wounds, managing burns, recognizing shock, and performing basic CPR and choking relief are all skills that will help keep you and others safe when professional help is out of reach.

Basic First-Aid Techniques

Understanding Wounds

If left untreated, a minor cut or scrape can lead to serious complications. Without access to proper medical facilities, infections can quickly set in, turning a simple injury into a life-threatening situation in a future without grids. The first step in wound care is understanding how to treat various types of injuries, ranging from superficial cuts to more severe gashes.

- **Cleaning the wound:** No matter the severity of the wound, the first thing you must do is clean it thoroughly to prevent infection. Use clean water to wash away dirt and debris. If available, you can disinfect the area with an antiseptic solution, like hydrogen peroxide or iodine. Keeping the wound clean is imperative, especially when antibiotics or advanced medical care may not be accessible.

- **Bandaging and dressing:** Once the wound is clean, you'll need to protect it from further contamination. If you have sterile bandages, use them, or improvise with a clean cloth or gauze. Ensure the dressing is snug but not tight, as you don't want to cut off circulation. Change the dressing regularly to monitor for signs of infection, such as redness, swelling, or pus.

- **Treating deep wounds:** Controlling the bleeding is the top priority for deeper cuts or lacerations. Apply direct pressure to the wound with a clean cloth or bandage. If the bleeding doesn't stop, elevate the wounded area above the heart if possible. Once the bleeding is under control, the wound may require stitching. While it's ideal to have sutures on hand, if you don't, butterfly bandages or even super glue can hold the wound edges together temporarily.

Knowing how to treat wounds effectively will help prevent a manageable injury from spiraling into a critical health issue. Swift and proper care is fundamental for staying healthy in a survival situation.

Managing Burns

Burns are another common injury in survival situations, especially when fire becomes a primary tool for warmth and cooking. Depending on the severity, burns can range from mild discomfort to life-threatening injuries. That is why you need to understand how to treat them correctly, as it can help minimize the risk of infection and long-term damage.

- **First-degree burns:** These burns affect only the outer layer of the skin and are marked by redness and pain, similar to a sunburn. So, cool the affected area immediately by running it under cool water for at least ten to twenty minutes. Avoid using ice; it can damage the skin further. Once cooled, apply aloe vera or an antibiotic ointment to soothe the skin and prevent infection.

- **Second-degree burns:** These burns penetrate deeper into the skin, often causing blisters. In addition to cooling the burn with water, it's important not to pop any blisters, as this can lead to infection. Cover the burn loosely with a sterile and nonstick dressing to protect the area while it heals. Keep an eye out for signs of infection as the burn recovers.

- **Third-degree burns:** These are the most severe type of burns and require immediate medical attention. They can destroy all layers of skin and may even damage underlying tissue. Managing third-degree burns is challenging, and your goal should be to stabilize the injured person until professional help can be obtained. Do not apply water to the burn, as this can lead to shock. Instead, cover the burn with a clean, loose cloth and monitor the person for signs of shock (discussed later in this chapter).

When managing burns, always prioritize cooling the burn quickly to reduce damage and infection risks. Having basic burn ointments and dressings in your emergency kit is a good preventive measure for any survival situation.

Recognizing Shock Symptoms

Shock is a life-threatening condition that can occur after an injury, trauma, or sudden loss of blood. It's crucial to identify the symptoms of shock early and respond quickly. Otherwise, untreated shock can lead to organ failure and death.

- **Signs of shock:** Symptoms include pale or clammy skin, rapid breathing, a weak but fast pulse, confusion, dizziness, or fainting. The person may also feel extremely thirsty or nauseous. These signs indicate the body is not getting enough blood flow to its vital organs.

- **How to treat shock:** The first step is to lay the person down on their back, if possible, and elevate their legs slightly to encourage blood flow to the heart. Keep the person warm with blankets or clothing, as shock can cause a sudden drop in body temperature. Reassure them and keep them calm. Anxiety can make the condition worse. If you suspect internal bleeding or a severe injury, try to immobilize the person to avoid further harm.

Basic CPR and Choking Relief

Cardiac arrest and choking are medical emergencies that demand immediate attention. In a gridless world, you won't have the luxury of waiting for an ambulance, so learning how to perform CPR and relieve choking is your only option.

- **CPR basics:** Cardiopulmonary resuscitation (CPR) is a lifesaving technique used when someone's heart has stopped beating. If you find someone unconscious and unresponsive, the first thing to do is check for breathing. If they are not breathing, start chest compressions immediately. Place the heel of your hand in the center of the person's chest and press down hard and fast—about two inches deep at a rate of 100 to 120 compressions per minute (think of the beat of the song "Stayin' Alive"). If you've been trained, provide rescue breaths after every thirty compressions, but if you haven't, focus on compressions only (Barrell, 2023).

- **Choking relief:** Choking is another common emergency, and knowing how to perform the Heimlich maneuver can prevent a tragedy. If someone is choking and unable to cough or speak, stand behind them and wrap your arms around their waist. Make a fist with one hand and place it just above their navel. Grasp your fist with the other hand and perform quick, upward thrusts into their abdomen until the object is dislodged. If the person loses consciousness, begin CPR immediately.

Fire-Making Without Matches

In a postapocalyptic world, the capability to make fire without modern tools, like matches or lighters, is one of the most important survival skills you can have. Fire offers warmth, protection, a means to cook food, and even a morale boost in challenging circumstances. Knowing how to create fire with what's available around you ensures you can stay warm, purify water, cook food, and signal for help if needed.

Let's explore some proven methods for making fire without matches, starting with the basics and moving into more advanced techniques:

The Hand Drill Method

The hand drill is one of the oldest and simplest methods for making fire. It uses friction to generate heat, which can then ignite a piece of tinder. Though it requires patience and practice, mastering this technique can be invaluable in a survival situation.

Materials needed:

- wooden spindle (a straight, dry stick)

- fireboard (a flat, dry piece of wood)

How to do it:

1. Create a small notch in the fireboard, and place some dry tinder (dry grass, leaves, or shredded bark) right next to the notch.

2. Place the spindle into the notch and spin it rapidly between your palms, pushing downward to create friction. As you spin the spindle, it will start to create heat, producing fine wood dust.

3. Keep spinning until the dust starts to smoke. Gently transfer the glowing embers to your tinder bundle and blow softly to ignite the flame.

Tips: The key to success with the hand drill is to use dry, soft wood, like willow, cedar, or poplar, and to be persistent with your effort. This method can be physically demanding, so prepare yourself for it.

The Bow Drill Method

The bow drill is a more efficient variation of the hand drill, and it's easier to maintain the spinning motion over a longer period. It's a classic fire-starting technique that can be used in almost any environment where you can find dry wood.

Materials needed:

- bow (a bent stick with a string or shoelace attached)

- spindle (similar to the hand drill)

- fireboard (with a small notch)

- socket (a smooth rock or piece of wood to press down on the spindle)

How to do it:

1. Wrap the bowstring around the spindle and place the spindle into the notch of the fireboard.

2. Hold the socket in your hand, pressing down on the top of the spindle to keep it steady.

3. Saw the bow back and forth, spinning the spindle quickly against the fireboard. The friction will create heat and eventually produce embers.

4. Transfer the glowing ember to your tinder bundle, blow gently, and watch as the flame ignites.

Tips: The bow drill is easier than the hand drill because it allows for greater speed and pressure. Make sure your bowstring is tight enough to keep the spindle spinning but not so tight that it's hard to saw back and forth.

Flint and Steel Method

The flint and steel method is a reliable way to make fire, especially if you have access to a few basic tools. This method involves striking a piece of steel against flint to create sparks that ignite a piece of char cloth or dry tinder.

Materials needed:

- piece of flint (or another hard stone like quartz)

- piece of steel

- tinder (such as char cloth, dry grass, or fine wood shavings)

How to do it:

1. Hold the flint in one hand and the steel in the other. Strike the steel against the flint at a sharp angle, creating sparks.

2. Direct the sparks onto your tinder, such as char cloth. When a spark catches, it will create a small glowing ember.

3. Gently blow on the ember to transfer it to your tinder bundle and ignite the flame.

Tips: Char cloth is a piece of cloth that's been heated without oxygen and is very good at catching sparks. You can make char cloth by placing cotton fabric in a tin with small holes and heating it in a fire until it turns black.

Fire Plow Method

The fire plow is another friction-based technique, but instead of spinning a spindle, you use a pushing motion to create heat.

Materials needed: two pieces of softwood—one as the plow (a sturdy stick) and the other as the base (a flat plank of wood)

How to do it:

1. Carve a groove into the fireboard (your base wood).

2. Place the tip of the plow (stick) into the groove and begin pushing it back and forth, creating friction.

3. As you push the plow, dust and heat will start to build up in the groove.

4. When you see smoke, add your tinder to the embers and blow gently to ignite the fire.

Tips: The fire plow is especially effective in tropical environments where wood is more likely to be soft and dry. Use a steady, firm pressure when pushing the plow to increase the chances of generating enough heat.

The Magnifying Glass (Solar Ignition) Method

If you're lucky enough to have access to a magnifying glass or even eyeglasses, you can use the sun's power to start a fire. This method works by concentrating sunlight into a small point of intense heat, which can ignite tinder.

Materials needed:

- magnifying glass, eyeglasses, or another convex lens

- dry tinder

How to do it:

1. On a sunny day, position the magnifying glass over your tinder, focusing the sunlight into a single, bright spot.

2. Hold the lens steady until the tinder begins to smoke.

3. Blow gently on the ember to ignite a flame.

Tips: This method only works during the day and requires a clear, sunny sky. You'll need patience, but once the sunlight is concentrated in a tight beam, it can ignite dry tinder relatively quickly.

Battery and Steel Wool Method

This method is particularly useful if you can access modern items, like batteries and steel wool. It's a quick and effective way to start a fire using the electrical current from the battery to ignite the steel wool.

Materials needed:

- battery (9V works best)

- steel wool

How to do it:

1. Stretch out a piece of steel wool, making it fluffy to increase the surface area.
2. Touch the battery terminals to the steel wool. The electrical current will heat the steel wool, causing it to spark and ignite.
3. Place the burning steel wool onto your tinder bundle and blow gently to get the fire going.

Tips: Always handle steel wool carefully, as it can catch fire quickly. Once it starts to spark, keep a close eye on it and make sure your tinder is ready to catch flame.

Navigational Skills Using Natural Landmarks

When modern technology, like GPS or compasses, is no longer available, learning to navigate using natural landmarks is your best survival option. Understanding the lay of the land, reading the environment, and being able to orient yourself without electronic assistance will help you ensure safety in a postapocalyptic world. This skill will help you find your way and sharpen your awareness of your surroundings, keeping you grounded and prepared.

Let's explore how to use natural landmarks to stay on course, from identifying key features to understanding how the sun, moon, and stars can serve as your guides.

The Importance of Landmarks

Natural landmarks are specific, easily recognizable features of the landscape that help guide you as you move through unfamiliar terrain. Unlike street signs or digital maps, these elements are permanent and can be found in most environments. Key natural landmarks can include:

- **Mountains or hills:** These large formations are easy to spot from a distance and can act as beacons, guiding you toward or away from certain areas.

- **Rivers and streams:** Waterways often flow in predictable directions, so following a river downstream can lead you to larger bodies of water or inhabited areas.

- **Rock formations:** Unique rock shapes can help orient you, especially in open areas like deserts or plains.

- **Forests or tree lines:** Large expanses of trees or changes in vegetation can serve as markers, especially in flat landscapes where other features might be limited.

In addition to major landmarks, smaller, subtler elements can help you maintain direction, such as an oddly shaped tree or a specific bend in a river. These features allow you to track progress and remain oriented in your surroundings.

Using the Sun for Direction

The sun is one of the most reliable tools for natural navigation. It rises in the east and sets in the west, making it a constant reference point for finding your way during the day.

- **Finding east and west:** In the morning, stand with the sun rising to your right, which is east. This means ahead of you is north, and to your left is west. At sunset, stand with the sun to your left, that's west. It signals that ahead of you is north, and to your right is east.

Another helpful method is to track the sun's shadow. Place a stick vertically in the ground and mark the tip of its shadow with a stone or another object. Wait about fifteen minutes and mark where the shadow moves. The first mark indicates west, and the second indicates east.

Let's understand it with the help of a scenario: You're walking through a dense forest. You can't see distant landmarks, like mountains, but you know it's mid-afternoon, and the sun is beginning to set. By keeping the sun on your left side, you can maintain a steady westward course without veering off-track.

Navigating Using the Moon

While the moon isn't as consistent as the sun, it can still be a valuable navigational aid, especially at night. Like the sun, the moon rises in the east and sets in the west, though its path is less direct depending on its phase.

- **Full moon:** During a full moon, the moon's rise and set times align more closely with the sun's cycle. It rises in the east at sunset and sets in the west at sunrise, giving you a reliable east-west orientation at night.

- **Crescent moon:** During a crescent moon, you can estimate direction by visualizing a line through the two points of the crescent. In the Northern Hemisphere, this line extended to the horizon points roughly to the south. In the southern hemisphere, it points to the north.

If you're traveling at night and the moon is visible, you can use its position to determine which direction you're heading. A line drawn through the tips of the crescent can guide your sense of direction, helping you navigate with more confidence even in the dark.

Navigating Using Stars

In the absence of sunlight or moonlight, the stars offer another way to find your bearings. While this method requires you having some knowledge of constellations, it's a valuable skill when all other natural cues are unavailable.

- **The North Star (Polaris):** The North Star is one of the most reliable direction indicators in the Northern Hemisphere. It's located almost directly above the North Pole, so if you can find Polaris, you'll know which way is north (Editors of EarthSky, 2024). To locate Polaris, find the Big Dipper (Ursa Major). The two stars at the end of the Big Dipper's "bowl" point directly to Polaris, which is part of the Little Dipper (Ursa Minor).

- **Southern Hemisphere Navigation:** In the southern hemisphere, you can use the Southern Cross constellation (Crux) to find the south. The longer axis of the cross points roughly toward the South Pole.

For example, imagine you're lost in a remote area, and night has fallen. By locating the North Star, you know which way is north and can adjust your path to head in the direction you need.

Using Waterways for Navigation

Water sources are another prominent feature when navigating using natural landmarks. Rivers and streams often lead to larger bodies of water or human settlements, and understanding how to read water flow can help you decide which direction to follow.

- **Rivers flow to the sea:** Rivers typically flow downhill and eventually lead to larger bodies of water, such as lakes, seas, or oceans. If you follow a river downstream, there's a good chance you'll encounter civilization or a place with more abundant resources.

- **Crossing streams and rivers:** When crossing a stream or river, note the flow direction, as this can help you maintain your orientation once you've reached the other side.

You come across a river while hiking through a wilderness area. You're unsure which way to go but remember that following a river downstream often leads to human settlements. You decide to walk alongside the river, staying alert for signs of life or clearer paths.

Identifying Changes in Vegetation and Animal Behavior

Nature itself can serve as a guide if you know what to look for. Subtle changes in vegetation or animal behavior can indicate where water or shelter will be located.

- **Vegetation as a water indicator:** Lush, green plants often grow near water sources. If you're in a dry area and come across a patch of green, there's a good chance that water is nearby.

- **Animal movements:** Animals, especially birds, can indicate nearby water or shelter. Birds tend to fly toward water at dawn and dusk, and observing their flight paths can lead you to water sources.

For example, you're walking through a dry landscape and begin to notice more green plants appearing as you continue. Following this shift in vegetation, you find a small stream that provides both hydration and a sense of direction.

Reading the Landscape for Shelter

Beyond navigation, natural landmarks can also guide you to places of shelter. In survival situations, knowing how to find or identify safe shelter locations is crucial.

- **Caves and rock overhangs:** In hilly or mountainous regions, caves or rock overhangs can offer immediate shelter from wind or rain.

- **Thickets and dense forests:** In forests, thick vegetation can shield you from the elements, though it's important to ensure it's safe from predators or flooding.

Imagine you're caught in a sudden storm while hiking. As the wind picks up, you notice a rocky outcrop in the distance. By heading toward this natural landmark, you will find shelter under a large overhang, protecting yourself from the worst of the weather.

Building and Setting Traps

Next, securing food will be your top priority. While foraging can sustain you for a while, hunting becomes necessary for long-term survival. This is where learning to build and set traps comes into play. Effective trapping allows you to capture small games without exhausting too much energy, which is essential when resources are scarce. Knowing how to construct traps from natural materials can increase your chances of success in harsh environments.

In this section, we'll explore some basic traps you can create and how to set them for maximum efficiency. From simple snares to more complex mechanisms, these traps can help you secure food even when you can't actively hunt.

Understanding Trapping

Before diving into the specifics, it's vital to grasp the basics of trapping. The goal is to use an animal's natural behavior against it, guiding it into a situation where it can't escape. Whether you're trapping a rabbit, squirrel, or other small game, the principles remain the same:

- **Know your target:** Different animals require different trap types. Small game, like rabbits or squirrels, are easier to trap than larger animals. Learn about the creatures in your area, their habits, and their movement patterns to set traps accordingly.

- **Placement is key:** Placing your trap in an area frequented by animals multiplies your chances of success. Look for signs, such as animal tracks, droppings, or chewed vegetation, to identify a good location.

- **Camouflage:** Animals are often wary of anything unfamiliar in their environment. To improve the effectiveness of your traps, camouflage them with natural materials. It can be leaves, grass, or sticks so they blend in with the surroundings.

The Basic Snare Trap

The snare trap is one of the simplest and most effective for catching small game. A snare consists of a noose made from wire, string, or vine that tightens around the animal's neck or body when triggered.

Materials: To make a snare, you'll need wire, strong string, or flexible vine. Thin, strong wire works best because it's durable and difficult for animals to chew through.

Construction:

1. Create a small loop at one end of the wire or string.
2. Run the other end of the wire through this loop to form a larger, adjustable loop. This is the part that will tighten around the animal.
3. Attach the snare to a sturdy object, like a tree or a peg driven into the ground.
4. Position the loop at the target animal's head height in a path it is likely to follow.

Placement tips: Place the snare on animal trails where you see frequent tracks or signs of movement. Ensure the snare is well-camouflaged with leaves or grass so the animal doesn't notice it until it's too late.

For instance, if you're in a forested area with lots of rabbits, look for rabbit trails in the underbrush. Set your snare along these trails, ensuring the noose is at the right height to catch a rabbit by the neck or body as it passes through.

Deadfall Trap

A deadfall trap uses a heavy object (such as a rock or log) to crush the animal when triggered. It's especially useful for catching slightly larger game like raccoons or rabbits.

Materials: You'll need a heavy object (rock or log), a stick or branch for support, and bait to lure the animal.

Construction:

1. Find a flat rock or log heavy enough to kill your target.
2. Set up a support stick in a way that holds the weight of the rock or log but can be easily knocked over.
3. Attach bait to the support stick so that when the animal touches or pulls it, the rock or log falls, trapping or crushing the animal.

Placement tips: Deadfall traps are best placed near animal burrows or feeding spots. Make sure the trap is stable but sensitive enough to fall when triggered.

Suppose you spot a raccoon near a riverbank where it regularly looks for food. You can place a deadfall trap in this area, using fish guts or other raccoon-friendly bait to lure it into triggering the trap.

Pitfall Trap

A pitfall trap is another straightforward method of trapping animals, especially if you're targeting larger game, like wild pigs. It involves digging a hole in the ground that's deep enough to prevent the animal from climbing out once it falls in.

Materials: All you need is a digging tool and natural materials to camouflage the pit.

Construction:

1. Dig a hole large enough and deep enough for your target animal. For small game, a few feet deep will suffice, while larger animals require deeper pits.
2. Cover the pit with branches, leaves, or grass to disguise it.
3. Place bait near or on top of the pit to attract animals.

Placement tips: Set pitfall traps near animal trails, especially those frequented by larger game. Make sure the pit is well-camouflaged and deep enough so the animal can't escape.

In a situation where you've noticed wild pigs in the area, a well-placed pitfall trap can be your best bet. Dig a deep hole along the trail they frequent, cover it with light branches and leaves, and wait for the pig to fall in while searching for food.

Trigger Mechanisms

For more advanced traps, adding a trigger mechanism enhances their effectiveness. A trigger is a delicate mechanism that, when disturbed, releases the trap, whether it's a snare, deadfall, or other contraption.

A simple snare trap uses a loop of wire or string that tightens when an animal walks through it. This type of trap can be set up quickly and is effective for catching rabbits, raccoons, and other small game. Here's how to create and use a basic snare trap:

Materials needed:

- length of wire, cord, or strong string

- sturdy support structure (like a branch or a tree)

- triggering mechanism (this can be a simple stick or a branch)

How to do it:

1. **Choose a location:** Look for animal trails, tracks, or areas where animals frequently pass. Setting the snare in a location with plenty of signs of activity will increase your chances of a successful catch.

2. **Prepare the snare loop:** Take your wire or cord and create a loop. Make sure the loop is large enough to accommodate the animal but tight enough to constrict when pulled. Typically, a six- to eight-inches in diameter loop works well for small animals.

3. **Position the snare:** Attach the loop to a sturdy support structure, such as a tree branch or a sturdy bush. You can use another piece of wire or cord to secure the loop to the support.

4. **Set the trigger:** To create a simple trigger mechanism, you can use a small stick to prop open the

snare loop. When an animal walks through the loop and pulls on it, the stick will dislodge, causing the snare to tighten around the animal.

5. **Camouflage:** To increase the effectiveness of your snare, consider camouflaging the area. Use leaves, grass, or other natural materials to cover the snare and make it less visible to passing animals.

How it works:

When an animal approaches the bait (if you choose to include some) or simply walks through the snare, it disturbs the setup. The disturbance causes the trigger stick to fall away, allowing the snare to close tightly around the animal's neck or body, securing the catch.

- **Spring pole snare:** In this setup, a bent tree or sapling is used as a spring. The snare is attached to the sapling, which is bent and held in place by a trigger. When the animal disturbs the trigger, the sapling snaps upright, tightening the snare.

The spring pole snare is perfect for areas with small, lightweight animals like rabbits. Using a flexible sapling, you can create a trap that snags the animal and lifts it off the ground, preventing escape.

Safety and Ethics in Trapping

While trapping is an effective survival skill, it's crucial to approach it with respect for both the animals and the environment. Set traps only when necessary and avoid causing undue suffering.

- **Check traps regularly:** Animals caught in traps can suffer if left for too long, so it's important to check your traps regularly to dispatch any captured game quickly and humanely.

- **Use only what you need:** Trapping for survival means using the resources you need to sustain yourself, not over-trapping or wasting the game.

Practice and Preparation

Like all survival skills, trapping needs practice. Setting up traps in a nonsurvival situation will help you gain confidence and fine-tune your skills for when you really need them.

- **Try trapping in different environments:** Practice setting traps in various locations, such as forests, meadows, and near water sources, to learn how animals behave in each environment.

- **Experiment with materials:** Get comfortable using a variety of materials, from wire to natural vines, so you're prepared no matter what resources are available.

Simply put, from the simplicity of a snare to the sophistication of a spring pole snare, each trap you master increases your chances of securing food when hunting isn't an option. By understanding animal behavior, perfecting your placement, and practicing regularly, you'll be well-prepared to thrive in a world where every resource counts.

Chapter 3:

Securing Clean Water Sources

Securing clean water should be your top priority when the grid goes down and taps run dry. In a gridless, postapocalyptic world, you can survive for weeks without food but only days without water. Knowing where to find water in nature—and how to make it safe to drink—can be the difference between life and death.

In this chapter, we'll explore how to locate natural water sources, the signs to look for, and how to ensure the water you find is clean enough to drink. Water is a critical resource for survival, so let's dive into the strategies you'll need.

Finding Natural Water Sources

Understanding the Importance of Water

Before we discuss finding water, it's crucial to grasp why it's so essential. Water regulates body temperature, aids digestion, and supports cellular function. Dehydration can lead to headaches, confusion, dizziness, and eventually death.

It's essential to locate and secure water within the first twenty-four to forty-eight hours of any survival situation.

- **Daily water needs:** The average adult needs at least 2 to 3 liters of water per day for drinking. This doesn't account for cooking or hygiene needs, which can add up quickly. In hot environments or if you're exerting yourself physically, you'll need even more (Gunnars, 2023).

- **Signs of dehydration:** If you notice dry mouth, dark-colored urine, or fatigue, dehydration could be setting in. In extreme cases, you may feel confused or weak. These are signals that your body is running out of water reserves, and it's time to act fast.

Finding Natural Water Sources

The good news is that water is present in many environments, even those that seem dry. The trick is knowing where to look and understanding the landscape. Nature will help you by providing a variety of clues if you know how to interpret them.

Rivers, Streams, and Creeks

One of the most reliable water sources is a flowing body of water. Rivers, streams, and creeks are generally easier to spot and often lead to other resources, such as plants and wildlife, that can help you survive.

- **Where to look:** Water always flows downhill, so head toward valleys or lower ground. If you find a small stream, follow it. You may discover a larger river downstream, which can give you more water and potentially can also provide food sources, like fish.

- **Signs of water:** Even if you can't see water right away, look for signs that it's nearby. Green vegetation is a good indicator, as plants, like cattails, often grow near water sources. Look for animal tracks as well—wildlife tends to gather around rivers and streams.

In a dense forest, the sound of running water can be your first clue. If you hear a distant babbling noise, move toward it. In some cases, animals, like deer or raccoons, can lead you to a nearby stream if you observe their movement.

Lakes and Ponds

Lakes and ponds offer still water, which can be more accessible than fast-moving rivers. However, stagnant water can harbor bacteria, so you'll need to purify it before drinking.

- **Where to look:** Lakes and ponds often form in natural depressions in the land. They're more common in forested areas or open fields. If you see a dip in the landscape, head toward it, especially if you notice lush plant life.

- **Water quality:** Be cautious with standing water. Algae, bacteria, or animal waste can sometimes contaminate ponds. If the water smells bad or has a greenish tint, you must purify it before drinking.

Springs

Natural springs are among the best sources of clean water. They occur when groundwater rises to the surface. Spring water is often fresh and pure, especially if it comes directly from underground.

- **Where to look:** Springs are typically found at the base of hills or mountains. Keep an eye out for areas where the ground seems particularly wet or mossy. Water seeping from rocks can be a sign of a spring.

- **Benefits of spring water:** If you find a natural spring, this water is often safe to drink without purification. However, it's always best to be cautious and purify any water in a survival situation if possible.

If you're in a mountainous region and notice wet, mossy rocks, this can be a sign of a natural spring nearby. Follow the moisture, and you might discover a reliable source of clean water.

Rainwater

Rainwater collection can be a lifesaver in certain survival situations. This method allows you to capture fresh water without relying on streams or lakes, especially in environments where water sources are limited.

- **How to collect rainwater:** Spread out a tarp, poncho, or any other large surface that can catch and funnel rainwater into a container. Even tree leaves can be used to channel rain into a collection spot.

- **Urban rainwater collection:** In a postapocalyptic urban setting, rainwater can be collected from rooftops using gutters or containers. Just be sure to filter and purify the water, as it may pick up contaminants from building materials.

Underground Water

In some cases, you may need to dig for water. This method is especially useful in dry or desert environments where visible water sources are scarce. Groundwater may be hiding just below the surface.

- **Where to dig:** Look for areas with green plants or animal tracks leading to a low spot in the landscape. Digging in dry riverbeds or near vegetation can sometimes reveal hidden water just a few feet underground.

- **Signs of water below ground:** Damp soil or mud can indicate water. Even in arid climates, you may find water by digging into shaded areas or low-lying parts of the terrain.

Making Water Safe to Drink

Once you've located water, the next step is ensuring it's safe to consume. Drinking untreated water, even from natural sources, can expose you to harmful bacteria, parasites, or viruses. You'll need to purify the water to avoid getting sick.

Boiling

Boiling is one of the most effective ways to purify water. It kills most pathogens that can make you sick, including bacteria and viruses.

- **How to boil water:** Bring the water to a rolling boil for at least one minute. At higher altitudes (above 5,000 feet), boil the water for three minutes, as water boils at a lower temperature in these areas.

- **What to watch for:** Boiling will not remove dirt, chemicals, or debris from the water. If the water appears cloudy or murky, you may need to filter it through a cloth or sieve before boiling it.

Filtration

Using a portable water filter is another method to ensure your water is safe to drink. Many survival kits come equipped with water filters that can remove bacteria, parasites, and even some chemicals.

- **Improvised filters:** In the absence of a manufactured filter, you can create an improvised filter by layering sand, gravel, and charcoal in a container. Pour the water through this makeshift filter before boiling to remove debris.

- **Benefits of filtration:** Filtration is especially helpful for removing larger particles or contaminants, like dirt, leaves, or small insects.

Chemical Purification

If you have access to water purification tablets or drops, they can quickly neutralize harmful pathogens in water. Iodine or chlorine-based tablets are effective, but the water may taste a bit odd afterward.

- **How to use purification tablets:** Follow the instructions on the packaging, usually adding one tablet per liter of water and waiting thirty minutes before drinking. Tablets are lightweight and easy to carry, making them a convenient option for survival situations.

For example, if you're by a slow-moving river that looks clean but isn't entirely trustworthy, you can filter the water through a cloth. It will remove any visible dirt, and then you can use a purification tablet to ensure it's safe.

The Long-Term Plan: Creating Sustainable Water Supplies

Once you've secured water for immediate survival, it's time to think long-term. In a gridless world, relying solely on finding natural water sources each day may not be sustainable. You'll want to create systems that ensure a steady water supply for the future.

- **Rainwater harvesting:** Build a permanent rainwater collection system using tarps, gutters, and storage containers. In areas with regular rainfall, this can provide a continuous supply of water.

- **Well-digging:** If you have the tools and skills, digging a well can provide a permanent water source. Wells can tap into groundwater, offering clean water without needing to constantly boil or filter.

Know that from recognizing natural signs of water to purifying and storing it, your survival depends on your ability to stay hydrated. By understanding the landscape and learning these techniques, you'll be better equipped to thrive, even when the grid is long gone.

Constructing Rainwater Collection Systems

In a world where clean water may become inadequate, the ability to harvest rainwater can be a lifesaving skill. Rainwater collection is a sustainable and practical method to ensure a steady water supply in urban and rural settings, especially when traditional water sources are contaminated or inaccessible. Constructing a rainwater collection system requires some basic materials and knowledge, but the payoff is a renewable resource that can provide water for drinking, cooking, hygiene, and even gardening.

Understanding Rainwater Harvesting

Rainwater harvesting entails collecting and storing rainwater for future use. It is an ancient practice used by many cultures and is particularly useful in areas that experience seasonal rainfall or have unreliable water infrastructure.

Why Harvest Rainwater?

- **Sustainability:** Rainwater is a renewable resource that can be collected with minimal environmental impact.

- **Self-sufficiency:** In a survival situation, relying on rainwater makes you less dependent on external water sources. Moreover, it gives you more control over your environment.

- **Cost-effective:** Once set up, rainwater collection systems are inexpensive to maintain and can lower your reliance on municipal water.

Rainwater is generally safe, especially when filtered. However, it can still pick up contaminants from surfaces like roofs, so purification methods (such as boiling or filtering) should be used before drinking.

Basic Components of a Rainwater Collection System

A simple rainwater collection system doesn't need to be complicated. You can make one from materials you likely already have or can easily find. Let's break down the essential components:

- **Catchment surface:** This is where the rainwater initially lands. Most often, this is the roof of a building, but you can also use tarps or other large surfaces.

- **Gutters and downspouts:** These channels direct the rainwater from the catchment surface into a storage container. If your roof already has gutters, you can modify them to feed into your system.

- **Storage container:** This is where the collected rainwater is stored. Barrels, large plastic containers, or even a makeshift tank can serve this purpose. Make sure the container is covered to keep debris and insects out.

- **First flush diverter:** This is an optional component that ensures the first few minutes of rainfall, which may carry dust, bird droppings, and other debris, are diverted away from your storage tank.

In a postapocalyptic scenario, you can use an abandoned house's roof as a catchment surface. By placing a barrel under the downspout, you can collect enough rainwater for basic needs, especially in rainy seasons.

Step-by-Step Guide to Building a Rainwater Collection System

Now that you know the essential components, here's a step-by-step guide to constructing your own rainwater collection system:

Step 1: Select a Catchment Surface

The roof of your house, shed, or any other structure with a sloping surface is ideal. Unlike some older shingles or treated wood, metal or plastic surfaces are preferable because they won't leach harmful chemicals into the water.

Tip: Clean the surface before the first rainfall to remove any debris or pollutants that might taint your water supply.

Step 2: Install Gutters and Downspouts

If your roof already has gutters, you can modify them to direct water into your storage system. If not, you can build a simple gutter system using PVC pipe or flexible tubing.

- **How to do it:** Attach the gutter to the edge of your roof and angle it slightly so water flows naturally toward the downspout. Position the downspout so it leads directly into your storage container.

Step 3: Set Up the Storage Container

Place your storage container at the end of the downspout. Make sure it's elevated slightly off the ground, which will help with water flow and prevent contaminants from entering. If possible, you can use food-grade barrels to avoid introducing harmful chemicals into your water.

- **Cover the container:** To prevent leaves, bugs, and other debris from contaminating your water, cover the top of the container with fine mesh or a fitted lid.

- **First flush diverter:** Install a first flush diverter, which directs the first few gallons of rain (which can be full of debris) away from the primary storage tank.

Step 4: Maintain and Monitor the System

Even a basic rainwater collection system requires regular maintenance. Keep the catchment surface and gutters clean, especially before major rainfalls. Regularly check your storage container for leaks or signs of contamination and ensure the water is treated or purified before drinking.

If you're living in a rural area post-disaster, you can use a large tarp as a catchment surface. By hanging the tarp between trees and directing it into a barrel, you can create a makeshift rainwater collection system to gather water during storms.

Maximizing Water Collection

To maximize your rainwater collection system, employ a few strategies to double the amount of water you collect.

- **Increase catchment area:** The larger the catchment area, the more water you'll collect. If your roof is small, consider setting up additional tarps or using other nearby structures.

- **Choose the right location:** Place your collection system in the area with the most rainfall. Monitor the direction of the wind and rainfall to confirm you're maximizing water collection.

- **Use multiple barrels:** If possible, set up a series of barrels or storage tanks connected by pipes. This will allow you to collect and store more water, especially during periods of heavy rain.

In a forested area where clearings are limited, you can place additional tarps around the perimeter of your camp. They can help you collect more water than relying solely on one roof or structure.

Purifying Collected Rainwater

While rainwater itself is generally clean, it can become contaminated once it hits surfaces like roofs or tarps. As a precaution, always purify the water before drinking. You can use these methods:

- boiling

- filtration

- chemical treatment

Once you have collected rainwater, you can use a simple portable filter to remove any bacteria or debris from the roof. This will ensure the water is safe for drinking and cooking.

Long-Term Considerations

For long-term survival, a rainwater collection system can be a crucial asset. However, you'll need to plan for periods of drought or low rainfall by conserving water and storing as much as possible when it's available. Consider incorporating backup methods for water collection, like digging wells or purifying water from rivers and lakes, to supplement your rainwater supply.

- **Conserving water:** Use water-efficient practices, like washing clothes in small batches, using water for multiple purposes (e.g., using leftover dishwater to irrigate plants), and covering your storage tanks to reduce evaporation.

In a dry season, carefully managing your rainwater collection and using it sparingly can mean the difference between thriving and struggling.

Storing Water Safely Long-Term

Rainwater collection systems can be particularly effective during the spring and summer months. Increased rainfall provides an excellent opportunity to gather substantial amounts of water. This is the ideal time to assess and expand your rainwater collection setup, ensuring it can handle higher volumes. Additionally, the warmer temperatures can facilitate quicker evaporation, which might necessitate more frequent checks on your stored water to maintain quality and prevent contamination.

Conversely, fall and winter can pose challenges. In many regions, precipitation may decrease significantly, leading to a potential shortage of fresh water. Freezing temperatures can also impact stored water; if your storage containers are exposed to extreme cold, they risk cracking or bursting. Therefore, you should insulate or move your water storage containers to a temperature-controlled environment during these colder months.

Storage Capacity Planning

When determining your storage capacity, you must account for immediate and long-term needs. Assess how much water your household consumes daily and consider the seasonal fluctuations in availability. For example, during warmer months, you may need to store more water to compensate for increased use, such as outdoor activities and gardening.

When planning your storage capacity, consider the following factors:

- **Household size:** Calculate daily water needs based on the number of people in your household, including any pets.

- **Usage patterns:** Consider how water usage may vary with the seasons—gardening in the summer, holiday cooking in winter, etc.

- **Emergency situations:** Factor in potential emergencies that could disrupt water supply, such as natural disasters, and ensure you have enough reserves to last at least two weeks.

Adaptability and Flexibility

Flexibility is your best friend in your water storage strategy. Regularly evaluate your water needs and storage capacity to adapt to changing circumstances. If you have excess water during the rainy season, you can consider redistributing it into smaller containers for easier use. Conversely, if you're running low during a dry spell, be prepared to adjust your daily consumption and rely more on alternative sources like filtration systems.

By understanding seasonal considerations and effectively managing your storage capacity, you can ensure a reliable supply of clean water throughout the year, no matter the challenges that arise.

Understanding Water Storage Needs

Before diving into the specifics of water storage, you need to understand how much water you'll need. The general recommendation is to store at least one gallon of water per person per day for at least three days. However, in a survival scenario, you may want to plan for much longer durations, especially if access to fresh water becomes limited.

- **Calculate your needs:** For a family of four, storing at least twelve gallons of water will be a starting point for a three-day supply. However, consider storing enough for a week or more, depending on your circumstances and available space.

Selecting the Right Storage Containers

Choosing the proper containers for water storage will guarantee its safety and longevity. Here are some tips for selecting appropriate containers:

- **Material matters:** Use food-grade plastic or glass containers specifically designed for water storage. Avoid containers that have previously held non-food substances, as they may leach harmful chemicals into the water.

- **Container sizes:** Smaller containers (like one-gallon jugs) can be easier to handle, but larger containers (like fifty-five-gallon drums) allow for more extended storage. Consider your space and how easily you can access the water.

- **Sealability:** Ensure your containers have tight-fitting lids to prevent contamination from dust, insects, and other pollutants.

- **Storage locations:** Ideally, store your water containers in a cool, dark place away from direct sunlight, which can degrade the plastic over time and encourage bacterial growth.

Preparing Water for Storage

Before storing water, it's important to prepare it correctly:

- **Clean your containers:** Wash your containers with hot, soapy water and rinse thoroughly. For extra assurance, you can sanitize them by using a solution of one tablespoon of unscented liquid bleach per gallon of water. Let the solution sit for a few minutes, then rinse well and let it air dry.

- **Use treated water:** Tap water is generally safe to store, as municipal supplies treat it for contaminants. If you're using well water or other sources, consider using water purification methods (like boiling or filtration) before storage.

- **Consider additives:** For long-term storage, adding a small amount of unscented liquid bleach (about 1/8 teaspoon per gallon) can help kill bacteria and prevent algae growth. Mix it thoroughly and let the water sit for thirty minutes before sealing.

Storing Water Safely

Once your containers are clean and filled, it's time to store them properly. Here are key points to keep in mind:

- **Labeling:** Clearly label each container with the storage date and contents. This helps you track freshness and identify containers when you need to rotate your stock.

- **Regular rotation:** Water doesn't expire, but the containers can degrade over time. Rotate your water supply every six months to a year and replace old water with fresh supplies. It will ensure you always have safe drinking water on hand.

- **Avoid freezing:** While storing water outside in winter may be tempting, freezing temperatures can cause containers to crack or burst. If you must store water in cold environments, you will need to see if your containers are insulated or kept in a temperature-controlled area.

Maintaining Water Quality

The quality of your stored water is paramount. You can keep it safe by following these strategies:

- **Regular checks:** Periodically inspect your water storage containers for leaks, cracks, or signs of contamination. If you notice any issues, replace the container and its contents immediately.

- **Smell and taste test:** Before using stored water, smell it and taste a small amount. If it has an off smell or taste, discard it and refill the container with fresh water.

- **Be aware of the environment:** Store your water containers away from chemicals, cleaning supplies, or anything that might contaminate the water.

Additional Storage Considerations

Depending on your needs and resources, you may want to consider a few additional strategies for water storage:

- **Rainwater collection systems:** As discussed in previous sections, rainwater harvesting can supplement your stored water supply, giving you an additional resource that can be filtered and purified as needed.

- **Water filtration systems:** Consider investing in portable water filters or purification systems that can treat natural sources of water (like streams or ponds) in case of an emergency. These tools can expand your ability to source water when needed.

- **Emergency water packs:** Keep small, portable emergency water packs (often found in survival kits) on hand for short-term situations. These packs are designed to have a long shelf life and can be an immediate resource during a crisis.

Chapter 4:

Food Production and Preservation

Imagine a world in which grocery store shelves are empty, and the familiar hum of refrigeration units has fallen silent. In this gridless landscape, food security becomes a pressing concern—one that requires creativity and resourcefulness.

Food production is not merely about growing crops; it's about understanding the rhythms of nature and working harmoniously within them. Whether you're planting a small garden or foraging for wild edibles, you'll discover that the ability to produce food can empower you and foster independence.

However, cultivation is only one piece of the puzzle. Preservation techniques are equally vital. They allow you to store surplus food for future use and ensure your hard work doesn't go to waste.

In the coming sections, we'll explore sustainable gardening, identify edible plants, learn the basics of hunting and fishing, and uncover preservation methods like drying and canning. By mastering these skills, you'll not only survive but thrive in a world stripped of modern conveniences. Let's embark on this journey toward food self-sufficiency!

Starting a Sustainable Garden

We all know that in a postapocalyptic world, growing food is not just a luxury but a necessity. A sustainable garden can give you fresh produce, reduce reliance on external food sources, and contribute to your overall self-sufficiency. Whether you're a seasoned gardener or a complete novice, starting your own sustainable garden can be both fulfilling and fundamental for survival.

Choosing the Right Location

The first step in starting a sustainable garden is selecting the correct location. Ideally, you want a spot that receives at least six to eight hours of sunlight per day, as most vegetables and fruits flourish in bright light. Look for a space that is easily accessible for regular maintenance but also offers some protection from harsh winds or extreme weather conditions.

Consider the following when choosing your garden site:

- **Soil quality:** Test your soil to determine its pH level and nutrient content. If your soil is too acidic or alkaline, you can amend it with organic materials, like compost, peat moss, or lime, to create an ideal growing environment.

- **Water availability:** Ensure you have easy access to water for irrigation. If possible, consider setting up a rainwater collection system to supplement your watering needs.

- **Space considerations:** Depending on your available area, you can opt for a traditional in-ground garden, raised beds, or even container gardening if space is limited.

Planning Your Garden Layout

Once you've identified the right location, it's time to plan your garden layout. A well-thought-out design will help maximize your space and yield. You can begin by sketching out your garden plan, considering the following elements:

- **Crop selection:** Choose crops that are well-suited for your climate and soil conditions. Heirloom varieties can be a great choice as they are often more resilient and better adapted to local conditions. Besides this, consider companion planting, which involves growing different plants together to enhance growth and deter pests. For example, planting basil near tomatoes can improve their flavor and deter insects.

- **Crop rotation:** To maintain soil health and reduce pest problems, practice crop rotation. This means planting different crops in the same area in subsequent seasons. For example, follow heavy feeders, like tomatoes, with nitrogen-fixing crops like legumes.

- **Vertical gardening:** If space is limited, consider vertical gardening techniques. Using trellises or wall planters allows you to grow climbing plants like cucumbers, peas, and beans, maximizing your growing area.

Building Healthy Soil

Healthy soil is the foundation of a productive garden. To create nutrient-rich soil, adding organic matter is your first step. Composting is an excellent way to enrich your soil. It offers essential nutrients while improving soil structure and moisture retention.

- **Composting:** Set up a compost bin using kitchen scraps (vegetable peels, coffee grounds, eggshells) and yard waste (leaves, grass clippings). Over time, microorganisms will break down this organic material into rich compost that can be added to your garden beds.

- **Mulching:** Use organic mulch, such as straw or wood chips, around your plants to suppress weeds, retain moisture, and gradually enrich the soil as it decomposes.

- **Natural fertilizers:** Instead of relying on synthetic fertilizers, consider natural options like fish emulsion, bone meal, or seaweed extract. These not only give nutrients but also enhance soil health.

Watering Wisely

Water management is a sensitive part of a successful sustainable garden. While plants need water to thrive, overwatering can lead to root rot and other issues. Here are some strategies to help your plants receive the right amount of water:

- **Irrigation systems:** Consider installing a drip irrigation system to deliver water directly to the root zone of your plants. This efficient method decreases water waste and the risk of fungal diseases caused by wet foliage.

- **Watering schedule:** Water your garden early in the morning or late in the afternoon to reduce evaporation. Check the moisture level in the soil before watering. For example, if the top inch feels dry, it's time to water.

- **Rainwater harvesting:** Use barrels or cisterns to collect rainwater from your roof. This conserves water and becomes a free source of irrigation.

Managing Pest and Disease

In a sustainable garden, know that you will need to manage pests and diseases without resorting to harmful chemicals. Let us learn some eco-friendly strategies:

- **Beneficial insects:** To help control pest populations naturally, attract beneficial insects like ladybugs and lacewings by planting flowers (like marigolds) that attract these helpful critters.

- **Organic pest control:** To manage infestations, use natural pest control methods, such as insecticidal soap or neem oil. Always test these solutions on a small plant area before full application.

- **Regular monitoring:** Regularly inspect your plants for signs of pests or disease. Early detection allows for swift action, which can prevent larger infestations.

Harvesting and Preserving Your Bounty

As your sustainable garden flourishes, know when and how to harvest your crops for maximum flavor and yield. You can employ these tips:

- **Know your crops:** Familiarize yourself with the harvest times for the plants you've grown. For example, tomatoes should be picked when fully colored and slightly soft to the touch, while leafy greens should be harvested regularly to encourage further growth.

- **Preservation techniques:** If you have an abundance of produce, consider preserving your harvest through canning, pickling, or freezing. These methods allow you to enjoy your garden's bounty long after the growing season has ended.

Embracing Community Gardening

In a postapocalyptic world, growing food can also be a communal effort. Consider joining or forming a community garden. These spaces foster collaboration, resource sharing, and camaraderie among gardeners. Community gardening enhances food security and builds social connections, which are invaluable in challenging times.

Identifying Edible Plants and Foraging

Foraging taps into ancient practices of gathering food from the wild. It is a sustainable way to supplement your diet. Many edible plants grow abundantly in forests, fields, and even urban areas, often overlooked by those unaware of their value. Foraging is not just a means of survival; it can also be a delightful and enriching experience.

Imagine strolling through a sun-dappled meadow, gathering fresh dandelion greens for a salad, or discovering wild berries to add a burst of flavor to your morning oatmeal.

Beyond the immediate benefits of food, foraging can also improve your overall well-being. It encourages mindfulness, physical activity, and a deeper appreciation for the environment. Plus, the thrill of finding and harvesting your own food can foster a sense of accomplishment and connection to the earth.

Understanding the Basics of Edible Plants

Before you embark on your foraging adventures, it's vital to familiarize yourself with some basic concepts of edible plants. Here are key categories to consider:

Common Edible Plants

Wild Greens: Many wild greens are nutritious and tasty. Some popular examples include:

- **Dandelion (*Taraxacum officinale*):** The leaves can be eaten raw in salads or cooked like spinach. The flowers can be used to make dandelion wine (MasterClass, 2022).

- **Purslane (*Portulaca oleracea*):** A succulent plant with a slightly sour flavor, purslane is rich in omega-

3 fatty acids and can be added to salads or stir-fries (MasterClass, 2022).

- **Lamb's Quarters (*Chenopodium album*):** Often considered a weed, lamb's quarters are packed with nutrients and can be used like spinach (MasterClass, 2022).

Wild Fruits and Berries: Many fruits can be foraged, offering a delicious addition to your diet. Consider:

- **Blackberries (*Rubus fruticosus*):** Sweet and juicy, they grow wild in many regions. Look for thorny vines in hedgerows and forests.

- **Elderberries (*Sambucus nigra*):** Both the flowers and berries are edible, although berries should be cooked to avoid toxicity.

- **Cattails (*Typha latifolia*):** The young shoots and immature flower spikes are edible and can be cooked or eaten raw.

Mushrooms

Mushrooms can be a fantastic source of nutrition, but they require careful identification. Some edible mushrooms include:

- **Chanterelles (*Cantharellus spp.*):** Recognizable by their golden color and trumpet-like shape, they have a distinct, fruity aroma (Filippone, 2023).

- **Morels (*Morchella spp.*):** These honeycomb-like mushrooms are highly sought after. However, ensure you know the difference between edible morels and their toxic lookalikes.

- **Porcini (*Boletus edulis*):** Known for its rich flavor, porcini can be found in forests and is great in soups and risottos (Filippone, 2023).

You can always consult a reputable guide or take a foraging class to learn how to identify mushrooms accurately, as some can be toxic.

Responsible Foraging Practices

As exciting as foraging can be, it's essential to do so responsibly to protect yourself and the environment. Here are some guidelines to follow:

Know the Law

Before you start foraging, familiarize yourself with local laws and regulations. Some areas may have restrictions on foraging in public spaces or protected lands. Always seek permission before foraging on private property.

Sustainable Harvesting

When foraging, practice sustainable harvesting techniques. This means taking only what you need and leaving enough for wildlife and future growth. Here are a few tips:

- **Harvesting techniques:** Use scissors or hands to snip off leaves for leafy greens rather than uprooting the entire plant. This allows the plant to continue growing.

- **Avoid overharvesting:** Only take a small percentage of what you find. For example, if you find a patch of wild berries, only harvest a third of the fruit to ensure the plants can continue to thrive and produce.

- **Respect wildlife:** Be mindful of local wildlife and their habitats. Avoid disturbing nests or burrows, and do not remove plants that provide crucial food or shelter for animals.

Be Mindful of Pollution

When foraging, be aware of your surroundings. Avoid areas that may be contaminated with chemicals, such as near roadways, industrial sites, or agricultural fields that may use pesticides. Always wash your foraged food thoroughly before consuming it.

Identifying Edible Plants: The Art of Observation

Successfully identifying edible plants entails keen observation and research. Here are some tips to help you become more adept at plant identification:

Use Field Guides

Invest in a reliable field guide specific to your region. Look for guides that include clear images, descriptions, and information about edibility.

Observe the Environment

Different plants thrive in various environments. Pay attention to the types of soil, sunlight, and moisture in the area where you find plants. Familiarize yourself with the ecosystems in your region. Knowing which plants grow together can help you identify them.

Study Plant Characteristics

Learn to identify plants based on their unique characteristics, such as:

- **Leaf shape:** Observe the shape, size, and arrangement of leaves. Are they broad or narrow? Smooth or serrated? For example, dandelion leaves are jagged and rosette-shaped.

- **Flowers:** Many edible plants flower, and their blossoms can help with identification. Notice the color, size, and shape of the flowers. For instance, elderberry flowers are small and white and grow in clusters.

- **Stems and bark:** The color and texture of stems and bark cannot be ignored for identification. For example, the stem of a wild carrot is hairy and grooved.

Foraging in Different Environments

The beauty of foraging is that edible plants can be found in various environments, from forests and meadows to urban areas.

Woodlands

Woodlands are often rich in wild edibles. Look for:

- **Wild garlic (*Allium ursinum*):** Easily recognizable by its garlic smell, wild garlic grows in shady spots and is great for flavoring dishes.

- **Fiddleheads:** The young and coiled fronds of ferns can be harvested in spring. They should be cooked before eating to avoid potential toxicity.

Fields and Meadows

Open fields and meadows are abundant with wild edibles. Seek out:

- **Chickweed (*Stellaria media*):** This nutrient-rich green is often found in fields and gardens and can be eaten raw in salads.

- **Wildflowers:** Many wildflowers, such as nasturtiums and violets, are edible and can add beauty and flavor to your meals.

Urban Areas

Even in urban settings, foraging can yield surprising results. Look for:

- **Fruit trees:** Many cities have abandoned or neglected fruit trees. Check for apples, plums, or cherries in parks or vacant lots.

- **Herbs and weeds:** Patches of clover, plantain, or wild mint can often be found in city parks and gardens. These can be added to salads, teas, or other dishes.

Foraging as a Social Activity

Foraging can be an enriching experience when shared with others. Consider organizing a foraging group with friends or family to explore local areas. This enhances safety since foraging alone can be risky. It allows you to share knowledge and enjoy the experience collectively.

Moreover, participating in local foraging workshops or classes can help you gain confidence and learn from experienced foragers. These gatherings sometimes give a wealth of knowledge, practical tips, and the opportunity to connect with like-minded individuals.

Basics of Hunting and Fishing

Hunting and fishing have been fundamental aspects of human survival for thousands of years. They allow you to tap into the natural food chain, providing fresh meat and fish while promoting self-sufficiency. Engaging in these activities can also lead to a sense of accomplishment and fulfillment as you learn to procure your food directly from the environment.

Benefits of Hunting

- **Nutritional value:** Wild game often contains fewer hormones and additives than store-bought meat. Deer, elk, and wildfowl provide lean protein, essential fatty acids, and vital nutrients.

- **Sustainability:** When done ethically and responsibly, hunting can contribute to wildlife management and conservation efforts, helping to maintain balanced ecosystems.

- **Physical activity:** Hunting requires physical exertion, from tracking and stalking to transporting your catch, promoting a healthy lifestyle.

Benefits of Fishing

- **Diverse food source:** Fishing offers a wide variety of protein options, including freshwater and saltwater species. Fish are rich in omega-3 fatty acids, beneficial for heart health (Ali et al., 2022).

- **Accessible:** Fishing can often be done in local ponds, rivers, and lakes, making it a more accessible option than hunting, especially for beginners.

- **Tranquility:** Many find fishing to be a meditative experience, allowing for reflection and a deeper appreciation of the natural world.

Basic Hunting Techniques

Understanding Game Animals

Familiarizing yourself with various game animals' behavior, habitats, and signs is crucial. Here are some common game species to consider:

- **Deer:** Often found in wooded areas and fields, deer are most active during dawn and dusk. To identify their presence, look for tracks, droppings, and trails.

- **Wild turkey:** These birds are social creatures that prefer open areas with nearby cover. Listen for their distinctive calls to locate them.

- **Small game:** Animals like rabbits, squirrels, and birds require different hunting techniques. Small game often frequents dense underbrush or tree lines.

Hunting Methods

There are various methods to hunt game, each requiring different skills and equipment:

- **Stalking:** This technique involves quietly approaching your target, and requires patience, stealth, and knowledge of the animal's behavior.

- **Still hunting:** This method involves moving slowly and quietly through an area, stopping frequently to listen and observe the game.

- **Calling:** Using calls or sounds that mimic the natural calls of animals can attract them. Hunters often use calls for species like turkey and deer.

Equipment Essentials

Having the right equipment is vital for a successful hunt. Here are some key items:

- **Firearms/Bows:** Depending on local regulations and personal preference, choose between rifles, shotguns, or bows. Ensure you are familiar with your weapon and practice regularly.

- **Ammunition/Arrows:** Use appropriate ammunition for your chosen weapon. Always check local hunting regulations regarding specific calibers and types of ammo.

- **Clothing:** Wear camouflage or earth-toned clothing to blend in with your surroundings. Layering is critical for comfort in varying weather conditions.

- **Hunting game:** Equip yourself with binoculars for spotting game animals, a hunting knife for field dressing, and a backpack for carrying gear.

Basic Fishing Techniques

Understanding Fish Species

Just as with hunting, understanding the behavior and habitats of fish is essential. Common fish species include:

- **Bass:** Found in freshwater lakes and rivers, bass are popular for their fighting ability and taste.

- **Trout:** Trout prefer cold, clean water and can be found in streams and lakes. They are often pursued using fly-fishing techniques.

- **Catfish:** Bottom-dwellers found in lakes and rivers, catfish are known for their size and are often caught using baited hooks.

Fishing Methods

Various techniques can be employed to catch fish, including:

- **Angling:** The most common method is using a rod and reel with bait or lures. This technique needs knowledge of casting and retrieving.

- **Fly fishing:** This specialized form of fishing uses artificial flies to imitate insects. Fly fishing requires specific equipment and techniques, including casting and presentation.

- **Trotlines and nets:** For larger-scale fishing, trotlines (a series of baited hooks on a line) or nets can be used, but these methods often require permits and adherence to local regulations.

Fishing Gear Essentials

Proper equipment is also needed for a successful fishing trip. Key items include:

- **Fishing rod and reel:** Choose a rod and reel combination suited for the type of fishing you'll be doing. Spinning rods are best if you are a beginner.

- **Bait and lures:** Live bait (worms, minnows) or artificial lures (spinners, jigs) can attract fish. You can also research the preferences of local fish species.

- **Tackle box:** Organize your hooks, weights, lures, and other gear in a tackle box for easy access during fishing trips.

- **Fishing license:** Ensure you have the necessary permits and licenses for your fishing activities, as regulations vary by region.

Safety Considerations

When engaging in hunting and fishing, prioritize safety for yourself and others. Here is some vital information:

Follow Local Regulations

Always abide by local laws regarding hunting seasons, bag limits, and fishing regulations. These rules protect wildlife populations and ensure sustainable practices.

Wear Safety Gear

Wear blaze orange clothing for hunting to ensure you are visible to other hunters. If you're fishing, wear a life jacket if you're on a boat and be aware of your surroundings.

Practice Firearm Safety

- If hunting with firearms, follow the four basic rules of gun safety:

- Treat every firearm as if it is loaded.

- Always point the muzzle in a safe direction.

- Keep your finger off the trigger until you are ready to shoot.

- Be sure of your target and what lies beyond it.

Stay Hydrated and Prepared

Whether hunting or fishing, bring plenty of water and snacks. Familiarize yourself with the area and carry a first-aid kit for emergencies.

Ethical Considerations

Hunting and fishing are not just about taking; they also involve respect for nature and wildlife. Here are some ethical practices to adopt:

- **Harvest responsibly:** Only take what you need and follow the principle of "leave no trace." Dispose of waste properly and respect wildlife habitats.

- **Educate others:** Share your knowledge of ethical hunting and fishing practices with others to promote conservation and responsible behaviors.

- **Advocate for conservation:** Support local conservation efforts and organizations dedicated to preserving wildlife habitats and resources.

Hunting and fishing are practical skills and fulfilling hobbies that can enhance your connection to nature. By understanding the fundamentals of these practices, you empower yourself to thrive in a gridless world. As you hone your skills, remember to approach hunting and fishing with respect for the environment, wildlife, and fellow practitioners. Whether you find yourself stalking game in the woods or casting a line on a tranquil lake, these experiences will enrich your life and strengthen your self-sufficiency. Embrace the journey of becoming a skilled hunter and angler, and let nature provide the sustenance you need.

Preservation Techniques Like Drying and Canning

In a world where access to fresh food may become limited, knowing how to preserve food is another invaluable skill that will come in handy. Drying and canning are two of the most effective techniques for extending the shelf life of your food, allowing you to make the most of your harvest or any foraged goods.

In this part, we will explore the intricacies of drying and canning, their benefits, methods, and practical tips to help you master these essential preservation techniques.

The Importance of Food Preservation

Food preservation is more than just a way to keep food from spoiling; it is about ensuring food security and maximizing resources in a gridless world. When infrastructure fails, relying on store-bought products may not be feasible. Here are some key reasons why preserving food is essential:

- **Reducing waste:** Food waste is a significant issue, with nearly a third of the food produced globally going uneaten. By preserving food, you minimize waste and make the most of your resources.

- **Seasonal availability:** Many fruits and vegetables are only available during specific seasons. Preservation allows you to enjoy these foods year-round, providing nutrition when fresh options may not be available.

- **Cost savings:** Buying in bulk when foods are in season and preserving them can save you money. Canned or dried goods can last for months or even years, making them a cost-effective solution for stocking your pantry.

- **Nutritional value:** Properly preserved foods retain their nutritional content, ensuring you maintain a balanced diet, even when fresh produce is scarce.

Drying: An Ancient Preservation Technique

Drying is one of the oldest methods of food preservation, dating back thousands of years. The process consists of removing moisture from food, which inhibits the growth of bacteria, yeasts, and molds. By reducing water content, you can significantly extend the shelf life of various foods.

Benefits of Drying

- **Lightweight and compact:** Dried foods are lightweight and take up less space, making them easy to store and transport.

- **Concentration of flavor:** Drying often intensifies the flavors of fruits and vegetables, making them a tasty addition to meals or snacks.

- **Versatility:** Dried foods can be used in a variety of dishes, from soups and stews to snacks and desserts.

Methods of Drying

- **Air drying:** This traditional method relies on natural air circulation to remove moisture. It works best in warm, dry climates. Hang herbs, fruits, or vegetables in a well-ventilated area out of direct sunlight.

- **Oven drying:** An easy way to dry foods at home, using an oven allows for more controlled drying conditions. Set your oven to the lowest temperature (around 140°F or 60°C) and place food on a baking sheet lined with parchment paper. Keep the door slightly ajar to allow moisture to escape.

- **Dehydrators:** A food dehydrator is a valuable investment for serious food preservers. These appliances provide consistent heat and airflow, ensuring even drying. Follow the manufacturer's instructions for optimal results.

Foods to Dry

- **Fruits:** Apples, bananas, peaches, and berries are excellent candidates for drying. Slice them evenly and consider dipping them in lemon juice to prevent browning.

- **Vegetables:** Carrots, tomatoes, and bell peppers dry well. Blanching vegetables before drying helps preserve color and flavor.

- **Herbs:** Basil, thyme, and rosemary are perfect for drying. Harvest herbs in the morning after the dew has dried for the best flavor.

- To keep dried foods fresh, store them in airtight containers away from light, heat, and moisture. Glass jars, vacuum-sealed bags, or mylar bags with oxygen absorbers work well for long-term storage. You can also label containers with the date of drying to keep track of freshness.

Canning: A Safe and Effective Method

Canning is an effective preservation method. It involves sealing food in jars and heating them to kill bacteria and enzymes. This process constructs a vacuum seal that prevents spoilage. There are two main canning methods: water bath canning and pressure canning.

Benefits of Canning

- **Long shelf life:** Properly canned foods can last for years without refrigeration, making them an excellent option for long-term storage.

- **Safety:** When done correctly, canning provides a safe way to preserve food. The heat during the canning process annihilates harmful microorganisms.

- **Taste retention:** Canned foods often maintain their flavors and textures, allowing you to enjoy seasonal produce long after harvest.

Canning Methods

- **Water bath canning:** This method is ideal for high-acid foods, such as fruits, jams, and pickles. Fill jars with prepared food, leaving headspace at the top, and seal with lids. Process the jars in boiling water for a specified time to create a vacuum seal.

- **Pressure canning:** For low-acid foods, such as vegetables, meats, and soups, pressure canning is required to reach higher temperatures that eliminate harmful bacteria. Invest in a quality pressure canner and follow the manufacturer's guidelines for safe canning practices.

Foods to Can

- **Fruits:** Can fruits in syrup, juice, or water. Popular options include peaches, pears, and applesauce.

- **Vegetables:** Canning vegetables, like green beans, carrots, and corn, allows you to preserve their flavors and nutrients.

- **Soups and stews:** Prepare hearty soups or stews and can them for quick, nutritious meals later.

Canning Safety Tips

- **Use proper equipment:** Invest in quality canning jars, lids, and processing equipment. Avoid reusing old lids, as they may not create a proper seal.

- **Follow tested recipes:** Stick to recipes from trusted sources, as they provide safe processing times and methods.

- **Check seals:** After canning, ensure all jars are sealed properly. The lids should not flex up and down. If any jars fail to seal, refrigerate and consume them within a few days.

To maintain quality, store canned goods in a cool and dark place. To keep your pantry organized, use a first-in, first-out system, consuming the contents of older jars first.

Combining Drying and Canning

While drying and canning are distinct methods, they can also complement each other. For example, you can dry fruits and vegetables nearing the end of their freshness before canning. This practice reduces waste and allows for a varied pantry filled with both dried and canned options.

Mastering preservation techniques, like drying and canning, can significantly enhance your food security in a gridless world. By understanding the processes, benefits, and best practices of these methods, you empower yourself to make the most of your resources, reduce waste, and enjoy nutritious meals throughout the year. As you embrace the art of food preservation, remember to experiment, keep learning, and share your knowledge with others. Your journey into self-sufficiency begins with these essential skills, ensuring you are well-equipped to thrive in any situation. Happy preserving!

Chapter 5:

Shelter-Building Essentials

In a postapocalyptic world, securing a reliable shelter can help you survive better. Your shelter is your physical structure. It also represents safety, comfort, and a refuge from the elements.

In this chapter, we'll explore the essentials of shelter-building, beginning with how to choose the best location for your new home in a gridless environment.

Selecting a Strategic Location

Choosing the right location for your shelter can significantly impact your comfort, safety, and overall survival. A well-selected site protects you from environmental dangers, provides access to vital resources, and enhances your security. Here are some key factors to consider when selecting a location:

- **Safety from natural elements:** Avoid building your shelter in areas prone to natural disasters, such as floods, landslides, or wildfires. Look for elevated ground to mitigate the risk of flooding, and steer clear of dead trees or unstable slopes that may pose a threat during severe weather.

- **Proximity to resources:** Your shelter should be close to essential resources, such as water, food, and firewood. Ideally, look for a site near a freshwater source, like a river, stream, or lake, while also ensuring the water is safe to drink. Also, assess the surrounding area for edible plants, foraging opportunities, or hunting grounds to sustain you long-term.

- **Natural protection:** Leverage natural features to enhance your shelter's protection. A hillside can offer insulation and shield against wind, while dense vegetation can act as a natural barrier against predators and intruders. Ideally, find a spot with natural cover while remaining open enough to allow sunlight for warmth and growing food.

- **Accessibility and mobility:** Consider how easily you can access your shelter and whether it allows for safe movement. You should overlook locations that need extensive climbing or traversing hazardous terrain. Also, your shelter needs to be easily reachable for gathering resources or potential evacuation (if the need arises).

- **Visibility and concealment:** While you want to be accessible to resources, you also want to minimize your visibility to potential threats. Seek locations that can become natural camouflage to obscure your shelter from prying eyes. This can include dense woods or a sheltered clearing surrounded by shrubbery.

Assessing the Ground and Climate

Once you've identified potential locations, assess the ground and climate conditions:

- **Soil quality:** The soil type can affect how well your shelter holds up against the elements. Do not build on sandy, loose, or waterlogged soils, as they can lead to instability or flooding. Opt for firm, dry ground that can support your structure.

- **Wind direction:** Understanding prevailing wind patterns in your area can help you position your shelter to maximize comfort. Ideally, construct your shelter to face away from harsh winds and elements, creating a more pleasant interior environment.

- **Temperature control:** Consider the temperature fluctuations in your chosen location. In colder climates, look for spots that receive sunlight throughout the day to keep your shelter warm. In hotter regions, opt for locations with shade during peak hours to maintain cooler conditions.

Creating a Blueprint

Once you've chosen a location, it's time to sketch a blueprint for your shelter. A simple plan lets you visualize how the shelter will fit into the environment and helps ensure you account for various elements. You can include:

- **Dimensions:** Determine how large your shelter needs to be. Consider the number of occupants and any necessary space for storage, cooking, or activities.

- **Materials:** Identify the materials available in your vicinity for construction. This may include wood, branches, leaves, mud, or rocks. Ensure you can gather enough materials to create a sturdy structure.

- **Entrance and Exits:** Plan for entrances that allow easy access while also considering security. A secondary exit can be crucial for emergency evacuation.

Building Your Shelter: A Basic Overview

With the location selected, the next step is to construct your shelter. There are various types of shelters to consider based on your resources and the environment. Here are some fundamental designs you can adapt to your chosen site:

Lean-To Shelter

A lean-to is a simple and effective shelter that can be constructed against a tree or rock. To build one:

1. **Materials:** Gather long branches or logs to create a frame and cover them with leaves, branches, or tarps for insulation.

2. **Construction:** Lean one end of the frame against a tree or solid surface at an angle, ensuring there is enough space inside for sleeping and storage.

3. **Insulation:** Fill in gaps with foliage or dry materials to improve insulation from the cold.

A-Frame Shelter

An A-frame shelter gives more space and stability than a lean-to:

1. **Materials:** Collect a number of sturdy poles for the frame and a larger collection of foliage or tarps for coverage.

2. **Construction:** Lean the poles together at the top to form an A-shape and secure the structure with more branches, creating two triangular sides.

3. **Roofing:** Cover the frame with leaves, grasses, or tarps. It will ensure the structure is waterproof and insulated.

Debris Hut

A debris hut is an excellent option for cold weather and uses natural materials to provide insulation:

1. **Materials:** Use a long, sturdy branch for a ridge-pole and gather smaller branches and debris for insulation.

2. **Construction:** Create a frame by propping the ridgepole between two supports and then covering it with branches, leaves, and grass, ensuring a thick layer for warmth.

3. **Space:** Create a small entrance at one end for easy access.

Earth Shelter

If you have the resources, consider digging into a hillside for an earth shelter. This method offers excellent insulation and protection:

1. **Digging:** Create a small trench or pit and build walls using mud, stones, or available materials.
2. **Roofing:** Cover the top with logs and soil for insulation, ensuring you leave openings for ventilation.

Types of Emergency Shelters

When faced with an emergency situation, reliable shelter can be the difference between life and death. Whether navigating a natural disaster, a postapocalyptic landscape, or a simple camping trip, knowing the types of emergency shelters available can help you make informed decisions and stay safe.

Let's explore various types of emergency shelters, from temporary structures to more permanent options, and consider the materials you can use to construct them.

Tents

Tents are the quintessential emergency shelter because of their quick assembly and portability. They come in various shapes and sizes, from small, one-person tents to larger family options. When selecting a tent, look for a model made from waterproof materials, ideally with a rainfly for added protection against the elements. Consider whether you need a tent that is easy to set up in low-light conditions or one durable enough to withstand strong winds or heavy rain.

Tarps

Tarps are incredibly versatile and can serve as an emergency shelter when combined with natural features like trees or rocks. They're lightweight, easy to pack, and can be set up quickly to create a makeshift shelter. You can use a tarp to create a lean-to, an A-frame, or simply drape it over a structure to block wind and rain.

If you find yourself in a survival situation and need to create a quick shelter, you can tie a tarp between two trees. This provides adequate protection from rain and wind. Elevating one side of the tarp allows for ventilation while keeping the interior dry.

Quinzhee (Snow Shelter)

Knowing how to build a quinzhee can be very useful if you ever find yourself stranded in a snowy environment. This type of shelter involves digging out a mound of snow and creating a hollow space inside. The insulating properties of snow provide excellent protection against cold temperatures, and it can be built with minimal tools.

Adventurers in the backcountry often use quinzhees when they're caught in unexpected snowstorms. This method keeps them warm and teaches valuable skills in snow construction and survival techniques.

Natural Shelters

Nature offers several types of shelters that can provide excellent protection. Caves, overhangs, and fallen trees can serve as natural shelters. When utilizing these options, check that they are safe from potential hazards like falling rocks or wildlife.

A-Frame Shelter

The A-frame shelter is a simple structure that gives excellent stability and protection. It consists of two slanted walls meeting at the top, forming an "A" shape. You can construct this type of shelter using branches, sticks, and foliage. The design allows snow and rain to slide off, reducing the risk of collapse.

Hikers and campers often construct A-frame shelters when they need quick protection from the elements. Using natural materials, they can create a safe space to rest or wait for rescue.

Lean-To Shelter

A lean-to shelter is another straightforward option that offers protection from rain and wind. It consists of a sturdy structure, such as a tree or large rock, with a slanted roof made of branches and foliage. This design allows for excellent airflow while keeping the interior relatively dry.

Wigwam (Teepee)

Traditionally used by Indigenous peoples, wigwams or teepees are cone-shaped structures made from wooden poles and animal hides or tarps. They are remarkably effective at retaining heat and provide a sturdy shelter against wind and rain.

Emergency Bivvy Bags

Emergency bivvy bags are a compact and lightweight alternative to traditional tents for those who prefer to travel light. These waterproof and windproof bags are designed to trap heat and can be easily packed in a backpack.

Hikers often carry bivvy bags as part of their emergency gear. In case of unforeseen circumstances, they can quickly deploy their bivvy bag to stay warm and protected from the elements.

Cargo Containers

In urban areas, cargo containers can serve as robust emergency shelters. They are insulated, weather-resistant, and can be modified to provide basic amenities. While not a traditional emergency shelter, their sturdiness makes them a viable option in specific scenarios.

Emergency Kits and Resources

While not a shelter in itself, having a well-prepared emergency kit can greatly enhance your shelter experience.

Include items like blankets, flashlights, first-aid supplies, and multi-tools to support your survival efforts.

Insulating Against Harsh Elements

When faced with the challenge of surviving in a gridless world, insulation is one of the most overlooked aspects. Proper insulation will protect you from extreme temperatures and help to maintain a comfortable living environment within your shelter. Whether you find yourself in a scorching desert, a frigid tundra, or a rainy forest, insulating against harsh elements is key to enhancing your chances of survival.

Let's delve into various methods and materials you can use to insulate your shelter effectively:

Understanding Heat Transfer

Before we explore insulation techniques, it's important to understand how heat transfer works. There are three primary modes of heat transfer: conduction, convection, and radiation.

- **Conduction** is the direct transfer of heat through materials. For instance, if the ground is cold, it will draw heat away from your body.

- **Convection** involves the movement of air or liquid. Cold air can enter your shelter, cooling it down, while warm air can escape.

- **Radiation** refers to heat loss through infrared radiation, which can occur even in well-insulated spaces.

To effectively insulate against these elements, you must address all three modes of heat transfer.

Natural Insulation Materials

Using natural materials can be an effective and eco-friendly way to insulate your shelter. Here are some options:

- **Straw and hay:** Due to their low thermal conductivity, both are excellent insulators. You can use straw bales to create walls or fill gaps in your shelter for added insulation.

- **Leaves and foliage:** Collecting dry leaves and layering them in your shelter can create an insulating barrier. Leaves trap air pockets and reduce heat loss.

- **Mud and clay:** Earth materials can help regulate temperature and provide insulation when applied as a thick layer over your shelter's walls. Some traditional building techniques incorporate straw and mud to create earth-sheltered homes. These homes maintain stable temperatures, providing comfort year-round.

Building Design Considerations

The design of your shelter plays a vital role in how well it can insulate against the elements. Consider these tips:

- **Shape:** A dome or A-frame shape minimizes surface area, which can reduce heat loss. This design allows snow and rain to slide off easily, preventing accumulation.

- **Elevated floors:** Building your shelter off the ground can help prevent heat loss through conduction. It also protects against moisture that could seep into your living space.

- **Air gaps:** Incorporate air gaps in your shelter's walls or roof. Compacted snow has many small air gaps. These gaps act as buffers against cold air, reducing heat transfer. In Inuit culture, igloos are designed with a dome shape and thick walls made from compacted snow. They become excellent insulation while allowing for ventilation (Hoyt, 2008).

Using Man-Made Insulation

If you have access to manufactured materials, these can also offer effective insulation as well:

- **Foam boards:** Lightweight and moisture-resistant, foam boards can be cut to fit your shelter's walls. They offer high insulation values and can be easily installed.

- **Reflective mylar:** This material can reflect heat into the shelter, lowering heat loss through radiation. It's especially effective when used as a lining on the inside walls or roof.

- **Old blankets and clothing:** Layering blankets, sleeping bags, or even old clothing can give added insulation. These items trap air and help retain body heat.

Sealing Gaps and Cracks

Air leaks can significantly compromise the insulation of your shelter. Take time to seal any gaps or cracks to minimize heat loss. Here are some methods to consider:

- **Natural sealants:** Fill gaps in walls and around doors with mud, clay, or a mix of straw and water.

- **Duct tape:** If available, duct tape can be used to cover small openings and leaks.

- **Snowpack:** In snowy environments, you can create a barrier by piling snow against the walls of your shelter. This not only acts as insulation but also helps to block wind.

Layering Techniques

Layering is a crucial principle in effective insulation. The more layers you have, the better the insulating effect. Consider these layering strategies:

- **Roof insulation:** If you're using a tarp or branches for your roof, add a layer of leaves or straw on top to enhance insulation.

- **Wall insulation:** Build walls using a mix of materials, alternating layers of natural insulation and man-made products to maximize thermal resistance.

- **Floor insulation:** Before placing your sleeping area, lay down leaves, straw, or grass on the ground. This will help create a barrier against the cold earth.

Maintaining Ventilation

While insulation is indispensable, it's equally important to maintain proper ventilation in your shelter. Stale air can lead to moisture buildup and create a breeding ground for mold. Here are some tips to achieve a balance:

- **Strategic vent placement:** Ensure your shelter has vents or openings near the roof to allow warm, humid air to escape while preventing cold drafts from entering the ground level.

- **Temporary openings:** When conditions allow, open flaps or doors for short periods to let fresh air in, particularly when cooking or during wet conditions.

Maintaining Structural Integrity

In a postapocalyptic world where survival hinges on the functionality and safety of your shelter, maintaining its structural integrity is paramount. Let's discuss the key strategies for ensuring your shelter remains strong, stable, and reliable, even under challenging circumstances.

Choosing the Right Materials

The foundation of your shelter begins with the materials you choose. Understanding the properties of different materials can make a big difference in the longevity and safety of your structure:

- **Wood:** A versatile and readily available material, wood is often used for framing and flooring. Choose hardwoods for their strength and durability, while softwoods work well for lighter structures.

- **Stone and earth:** Natural materials, like stone and earth, provide excellent durability and insulation. Building stone walls can offer structural strength and thermal mass, helping regulate temperatures.

- **Metal:** If you have access to metal sheets or scraps, these can be used for roofing or siding. Metal is fire-resistant and can protect against harsh weather but may require additional insulation.

Foundation Considerations

A solid foundation is a must for the stability of your shelter. Here are some tips to ensure your shelter is securely anchored:

- **Level ground:** Choose a flat, stable area to build your shelter. Avoid places prone to flooding, such as low-lying areas or near water sources.

- **Digging deep:** If possible, dig footings that go below the frost line to prevent shifting because of freeze-thaw cycles. This depth helps maintain stability regardless of temperature changes.

- **Drainage solutions:** Ensure your foundation has proper drainage to avoid water pooling, which can weaken your structure over time. Creating a slight slope away from the shelter can help channel rainwater away.

Reinforcement Techniques

Reinforcing your shelter can help it withstand high winds, heavy snowfall, and other environmental stresses:

- **Cross bracing:** Use diagonal bracing within walls to increase strength and stability. This technique distributes forces more evenly, reducing the risk of wall collapse.

- **Strapping and anchoring:** Secure roof rafters and wall frames using metal straps or heavy-duty rope to keep them anchored during storms. This method is especially important in areas prone to high winds.

- **Temporary supports:** While building, use temporary supports (like props or braces) to hold up sections until they are fully secured. This ensures no part of the structure sags or shifts during construction.

Regular Maintenance Checks

Once your shelter is built, focus on regular maintenance, as it is vital to preserving its integrity:

- **Inspect for damage:** Frequently check for any signs of wear or damage, such as cracks in walls, leaks in the roof, or weakened supports. Address these issues promptly to prevent further deterioration.

- **Reapply treatments:** If you've treated wood for pests or weatherproofed your shelter, make sure to reapply these treatments as necessary to prolong the life of the materials.

- **Clear debris:** Regularly clear away debris and vegetation around your shelter to prevent moisture buildup and reduce the risk of pest infestations.

Adapting to Environmental Changes

Your shelter may face challenges from shifting weather patterns or natural disasters in a dynamic environment. Being adaptable is vital:

- **Flexible design:** Consider building a shelter that can be easily modified or expanded. For example, structures that can be added onto or reconfigured allow you to adapt to changing needs or conditions.

- **Reinforcement for seasons:** Prepare your shelter for seasonal changes by reinforcing it in advance. For instance, add extra support for winter snow loads or a layer of ventilation for heat during summer months.

- **Emergency plans:** Have a contingency plan for emergencies such as floods, earthquakes, or wildfires. When you know how to evacuate quickly, your shelter becomes lifesaving.

Creating a Safe Environment Inside

The interior of your shelter is just as important as the exterior. Maintaining a safe and functional interior contributes to overall structural integrity:

- **Organized layout:** Keep the interior organized to prevent accidents and make the best use of space. Store heavy items low to the ground to prevent them from falling and causing injury.

- **Ventilation:** Ensure your shelter has adequate ventilation to prevent moisture buildup and improve air quality. This will help reduce the risk of mold and maintain a healthy living environment.

- **Emergency supplies:** Keep emergency supplies and tools accessible and organized. Having these on hand can help you address any structural issues quickly.

Chapter 6:

Self-Defense and

Security Measures

In a postapocalyptic world, we cannot overlook the value of self-defense and security. In the absence of modern law enforcement or the stability of societal order, it becomes a necessity to be prepared for potential threats.

In this chapter, we will focus on assessing these threats and creating primitive weapons to defend ourselves in the gridless future.

Evaluating Potential Threats

When society collapses and infrastructure breaks down, threats will likely emerge from a variety of sources. Evaluating potential threats is a central part of your security strategy, helping you stay one step ahead of any danger.

Human Threats

In a postapocalyptic environment, societal collapse can result in desperation, and people may resort to violence or theft to meet their basic needs. This makes human threats one of the most unpredictable.

- **Warning signs:** Keep an eye out for suspicious behavior, such as strangers approaching your shelter in large groups or people repeatedly scouting your location. Even small groups can pose a threat if they are armed or desperate.

- **Securing perimeters:** Setting up a clear boundary around your home or shelter can deter unwanted visitors. Simple measures, like creating visual barriers (a natural fence made from branches), can make it clear that your space is defended. If possible, position your shelter in a hidden or hard-to-reach location, reducing its visibility to passersby.

Animal Threats

Without urban structures, animals will likely roam freely, and their behavior can become more aggressive as they struggle to find food and shelter. While some animals can be a food source, others can be a source of danger.

- **Recognizing animal habits:** Understanding the patterns of local wildlife can help you prepare for potential threats. If you're in an area with large predators, like bears or wolves, you'll need to secure your shelter and food stores to avoid attracting them.

- **Setting up barriers:** Besides securing your shelter, setting up early warning systems, such as noise traps or barriers, can alert you to the presence of both animals and humans. For example, hanging metal cans from a string around your camp can create noise when they are disturbed, giving you extra time to respond to threats.

Environmental Hazards

Threats aren't limited to living creatures. In a gridless world, natural hazards, like storms, floods, or wildfires, become more dangerous without modern early warning systems.

- **Stay vigilant:** Regularly assess the environment for any signs of changing weather patterns or other natural dangers. Relocating your shelter before a flood or reinforcing it against high winds can help you.

By learning to evaluate threats from humans, animals, and nature, you'll be better prepared to secure your space and defend against potential dangers.

Crafting Primitive Weapons

Meanwhile, you will need to know how to craft primitive weapons, as they will give you a significant advantage. These tools can be crafted from materials readily available in nature or salvaged from abandoned buildings. Although not as powerful as modern weaponry, they can be effective in self-defense and hunting.

Spears

A spear is one of the simplest yet most effective weapons you can craft. It can be used for defense, hunting, and keeping threats at a distance.

- **Crafting a spear:** To make a spear, find a sturdy and straight branch about six to eight feet long. Sharpen one end using a knife or rock, or attach a metal or stone tip to improve its effectiveness. If you have access to fire, harden the sharpened end by holding it over the flames, which will make the wood more durable.

Bows and Arrows

A bow and arrow set means range, and range can allow you to engage threats from a safer distance. While more complex to craft, it is a valuable tool for self-defense and hunting.

- **Making a bow:** Look for a strong and flexible branch for the bow, about as tall as you are. The wood should bend without breaking. Use a sturdy cord, like paracord or sinew, to string the bow. For arrows, find straight sticks and sharpen one end. If possible, attach arrowheads made from sharpened metal or stone.

- **Hunting and defense:** While a bow takes practice to use effectively, it's a reliable weapon that can provide you with food or serve as protection. Learning to craft and shoot arrows is a beneficial survival skill in any postapocalyptic scenario.

Slingshots

A slingshot is also a simple but effective weapon, particularly for smaller game animals or as a deterrent. It can be easily constructed and used with minimal materials.

- **Crafting a slingshot:** To make a slingshot, you need to find a Y-shaped branch. Use sturdy elastic material, like rubber bands or strips from old tires, to create the launching mechanism. Stones or small metal objects can serve as ammunition, making the slingshot a versatile tool for hunting and defense.

Clubs and Bludgeons

Simple, blunt weapons, like clubs, are easy to make and can be highly practical in close combat situations.

- **Crafting a club:** Look for a thick and heavy branch or piece of metal pipe that can be comfortably held in one hand. You can modify the head by adding nails, spikes, or other sharp objects to enhance its damage potential. Clubs don't require much skill to use, making them a practical choice for immediate self-defense.

Setting Up Defensive Perimeters

A well-thought-out defensive perimeter is your first line of defense against unwanted visitors, be they human or animal. It's about making your living area harder to access while giving yourself the time and opportunity to react to any threats.

Physical Barriers

One of the most impactful ways to deter intruders is to set up physical barriers around your shelter. Even simple constructions can discourage people from approaching your space.

- **Fencing and barricades:** If you have access to building materials, such as wood, metal scraps, or even stones, constructing a fence or barricade around your perimeter is a great option. Make sure your barrier is high enough to make climbing over difficult. Natural fences made from thorny bushes or dense shrubs can also act as a deterrent.

- **Creating layers:** Don't rely on a single line of defense. Set up multiple layers, such as placing a wall of debris a few feet outside your main fence or stringing up tripwire traps that make noise when triggered. Each layer forces intruders to slow down, giving you more time to prepare for an encounter.

Camouflage and Concealment

Sometimes, the best defense is staying hidden. If your shelter blends into its environment, it's less likely to attract attention.

- **Natural camouflage:** To disguise your shelter, use natural materials like dirt, leaves, and branches. In a wooded area, for example, weaving branches and vines into the structure of your shelter can make it look like part of the landscape.

- **Avoiding direct paths:** Don't create a clear and visible pathway to your home. If possible, situate your shelter in a hard-to-reach spot, like a hilltop or a dense forest, making it difficult for people to stumble upon your space accidentally. Cover any trails you create by walking in different patterns each time or using leaves to disguise tracks.

Setting Up Early Warning Systems

An early warning system can be as simple as a tripwire or a line of noisy cans strung together. It's not about creating an impenetrable fortress but giving yourself the chance to know when someone or something is approaching.

- **Noisemakers:** Hang small metal objects, like cans or bells, connected by a thin wire or string around your perimeter. If disturbed, these items will create noise, alerting you to movement near your shelter.

- **Tripwires:** A tripwire placed along common access points can also serve as an early alert system. Run a thin cord across a path at ankle height, tying it to cans, bells, or other noisemakers. As soon as someone trips over the wire, you'll hear it.

Lighting

At night, your sense of sight is reduced, and that's when intruders are most likely to approach. To counter this, use lighting to disorient potential threats.

- **Controlled lighting:** Set up solar-powered or battery-operated lights around your perimeter to illuminate potential entry points. However, avoid placing them too close to your shelter, as you don't want to make yourself an easy target. By keeping the lights outside your main area, you can see threats coming without being seen yourself.

Learning Self-Defense Techniques

While a strong perimeter can deter many threats, it won't stop all of them. Knowing how to defend yourself physically is just as important. In a gridless world, self-defense becomes a lifesaving skill, ensuring you can protect yourself from harm when confronted with danger.

Basic Hand-to-Hand Combat

Even without formal martial arts training, understanding a few basic hand-to-hand combat techniques can make a huge difference. Know that your goal isn't to fight but to incapacitate an attacker long enough for you to escape.

- **Strikes to vulnerable areas:** The eyes, nose, throat, and groin are some of the most vulnerable areas of the human body. In a self-defense situation, aim for these areas to disable your attacker quickly. A jab to the eyes or a strong kick to the groin can buy you the time you need to get away.

- **Using your environment:** Look for objects around you that can be used as weapons—rocks, branches, or even dirt to throw in an attacker's face. Survival situations often call for improvisation, and anything can become your weapon if used correctly.

Defensive Posture and Escape

The next important step is knowing how to position yourself and when to retreat. The goal of self-defense is to neutralize the threat and remove yourself from the danger zone.

- **Keep your guard up:** When facing an opponent, stay in a defensive posture with your arms raised to protect your face and chest. Keep your feet shoulder-width apart and try to remain balanced so you can move quickly if needed.

- **Escape routes:** Look at your surroundings and know your escape routes. If an encounter escalates, your best option may be to flee rather than fight, especially if your attacker is armed or physically stronger.

Training with Improvised Weapons

In a world without modern conveniences, you may need to rely on simple and everyday objects as weapons. Learn how to make and wield these improvised weapons effectively.

- **Clubs and sticks:** A heavy stick or club is one of the simplest weapons. Focus on swinging for vulnerable areas, such as the knees, ribs, or head. Practice with these makeshift weapons to improve your accuracy and control.

- **Knives and sharp objects:** If you have a knife, learn how to use it defensively. Holding the knife in a reverse grip (with the blade pointing downward) can give you better control and leverage in a close-quarters fight. Always aim to protect yourself rather than going on the offensive unless absolutely necessary.

Chapter 7:

Fostering Mental Resilience

You might be thinking that surviving in a world without the safety nets of modern society seems quite challenging. This thinking alone is enough to make you feel less confident and discouraged. At such times, mental resilience becomes your next survival skill.

When faced with uncertainty, stress, and isolation, fostering mental strength can help you keep moving forward. This chapter is all about learning strategies to manage stress in crises.

Managing Stress in Crises

Stress can be overwhelming in a postapocalyptic world. With every day bringing new dangers and uncertainties, it's easy to get caught up in fear, panic, or despair. Learning to manage this stress is key to maintaining focus and making clear decisions when it matters most.

Understanding the Impact of Stress

Stress is a natural response to danger, but too much of it over prolonged periods can wear you down, both mentally and physically. It can impair your judgment, cause fatigue, and even weaken your immune system. Recognizing the signs of stress early on is the first step in managing it.

- **Common signs of stress:** Irritability, difficulty concentrating, trouble sleeping, or feeling overwhelmed are all common reactions. These symptoms can escalate quickly in a survival situation, so it's important to be mindful of them.

- **Physical impact:** Chronic stress affects your body's ability to function. For example, elevated levels of the hormone cortisol can increase the risk of high blood pressure and lower your immunity, making you more susceptible to illness, a serious risk when medical care is scarce.

Breathing and Grounding Techniques

When you're in a crisis, your body's fight-or-flight response kicks in, sometimes making it difficult to think clearly. One of the fastest ways to regain focus is through breathing and grounding exercises.

- **Deep breathing:** Taking deep, slow breaths helps reduce immediate feelings of panic. When you feel anxiety rising, focus on breathing in through your nose for a count of four, holding for four seconds, and exhaling slowly through your mouth for another four.

This technique calms the nervous system and helps lower stress levels.

- **Grounding techniques:** Grounding exercises help pull your mind away from overwhelming thoughts. A simple one to try is the 5-4-3-2-1 method: Identify five things you can see, four things you can touch, three things you can hear, two things you can smell, and one thing you can taste. It helps you stay present in the moment instead of being consumed by anxiety.

Establishing Routine Amid Chaos

In the absence of normal daily life, creating a personal routine can provide much-needed structure and stability. Even small, repetitive tasks can give you a sense of control.

- **Start with basics:** Tasks like preparing meals, organizing your shelter, or gathering supplies can become part of a daily routine. These actions not only ensure your basic needs are met but also offer mental relief by focusing on practical tasks.

- **Set small goals:** While long-term plans may seem difficult in a chaotic world, setting small, achievable goals can keep your mind focused. Whether it's improving your shelter, finding new water sources, or practicing a survival skill, accomplishing these goals boosts morale.

Seeking Connection

Humans are social creatures, and isolation in a post-grid world can worsen stress. Whenever possible, seek connection with others for emotional support and collaboration in survival efforts.

Building a Positive Outlook

Maintaining a positive mindset in dire circumstances can feel impossible, but it's one of the most effective ways to build long-term mental resilience. It doesn't mean ignoring the reality of your situation but finding ways to foster hope and motivation even when the outlook seems bleak.

Cultivating Gratitude

Gratitude can be a powerful tool for mental resilience. Even in the harshest environments, there are always small things to appreciate: fresh air, a safe shelter, or a successful hunt. Focusing on what you have rather than what you lack can shift your mindset from despair to possibility.

Take a moment each day to think about three things you're grateful for, no matter how small they seem. This simple habit can help you build a more optimistic outlook over time and counterbalance negative thoughts.

Adopting a Growth Mindset

A growth mindset is the belief that you can improve and learn from challenges rather than being defeated by them. This is essential when you're faced with obstacles that seem insurmountable.

Visualizing Success

Mental imagery can be a powerful tool for building resilience. When you visualize yourself succeeding in difficult situations, you're mentally rehearsing how to cope when those situations arise.

Spend a few minutes each day imagining yourself overcoming obstacles. It can be navigating dangerous terrain, building a fire, or finding food.

Picture the steps you would take and the feeling of accomplishment when you succeed. This exercise will help you build mental confidence and preparedness.

Celebrating Small Wins

When life is stripped down to survival, it's essential to acknowledge and celebrate every victory, no matter how small. These moments keep hope alive and motivate you to keep pushing forward.

Did you manage to purify the water today? Did you start a fire on your own for the first time? Each of these is an achievement that moves you closer to long-term survival. Celebrating small wins reinforces your progress and keeps your spirits high.

Creating Purpose in a Survival Situation

Trying to maintain a positive outlook is having a sense of purpose. In a gridless world, your sense of purpose has the potential to shift from work or societal roles to survival and care for others. When it feels like everything is falling apart, you need to find purpose in caring for yourself or others. Whether it's teaching someone a new skill, protecting a loved one, or simply continuing to survive, these acts of purpose provide a mental anchor.

Techniques for Overcoming Fear

Fear is a natural and inevitable response to the unknown, especially in survival situations where danger feels constant. However, if left unchecked, fear can paralyze you and prevent you from making clear decisions. Overcoming fear doesn't mean ignoring it but learning how to manage and channel it into productive action.

One of the first steps to overcoming fear is recognizing it for what it is. It is a biological response meant to protect you. It's important to acknowledge that fear is not inherently bad. In fact, it sharpens your senses and prepares your body to respond to threats. But letting it control you can lead to poor decision-making, unnecessary risks, or even inaction. By understanding this, you can start to take small steps to harness that energy and put it to use.

A practical technique for overcoming fear is focusing on what you can control. When faced with overwhelming uncertainty, narrowing your attention to immediate tasks gives you a sense of empowerment. For instance, suppose you're worried about an impending storm while your shelter isn't fully built. Instead of panicking, focus on what you can do right now (reinforcing weak spots or gathering additional materials). By breaking down larger fears into manageable actions, you're addressing the fear and reducing its intensity.

Breathing and mindfulness techniques can also help reduce the physiological symptoms of fear, such as a rapid heartbeat or a racing mind. When you're caught up in fear, it often stems from what-if scenarios. By centering yourself in the present, you can concentrate on the tangible and real challenges at hand.

Lastly, remember that fear diminishes with experience. The more familiar you become with your environment and survival tasks, the less room fear has to take hold. Repetition of basic skills, like fire-making or shelter-building, turns them into second nature, so when the stakes are high, you can rely on muscle memory instead of panic. Practice and preparation are the ultimate antidotes to fear.

Establishing Routines for Stability

Establishing routines is one of the most effective ways to create a sense of stability in a chaotic environment where normalcy has crumbled. Routines provide structure, and with structure comes a psychological sense of safety. When every day feels unpredictable, routines give you something familiar to rely on.

One of the most important reasons for establishing routines is that they conserve mental energy. In survival situations, decisions can become overwhelming, especially when resources are limited and time is of the essence. By setting routines, you eliminate the need for decision-making around daily tasks. For example, creating a schedule for tasks like gathering water, maintaining your shelter, or preparing food helps streamline your efforts and makes your day more manageable. In the long run, this reduces cognitive fatigue, leaving you better equipped to deal with new challenges.

Routine also helps to manage stress. Knowing that certain aspects of your day are predictable allows you to feel a greater sense of control, which is incredibly important when so much of your situation is outside your grasp. Even simple routines, like waking up at the same time each day, doing a quick safety check of your surroundings, or dedicating a few minutes to organizing your tools, can bring much-needed order to an otherwise unstable existence.

Food preparation is an example of how routine stabilizes your mindset. By setting a consistent meal schedule, you eliminate the guesswork and anxiety of when and what you will eat next. In a survival context, predictability is not just about staying nourished but also about maintaining morale.

Routines also reinforce a sense of progress. In a situation where it feels like you're just trying to survive day by day, routine tasks give you measurable goals to accomplish. Each small, repetitive task adds up over time, whether it's fortifying your shelter, building up food reserves, or mastering a new skill like fishing. Seeing that progression keeps you motivated and reminds you that you are still moving forward even in the harshest conditions.

Another key benefit of routine is its impact on group dynamics if you're not alone. Routines create predictability for everyone involved, fostering cooperation and reducing conflict. If everyone knows when and how specific tasks will be done, there is less room for disagreement, which is essential in maintaining harmony within a group under pressure.

In sum, establishing routines in a postapocalyptic world is about creating pockets of control in an environment where control is difficult to come by. It's a way of organizing both your time and mind, giving you the mental bandwidth to address more significant challenges while ensuring that the basics are consistently met. Over time, these routines will become the foundation upon which you build your survival strategy, helping you thrive even in the most uncertain times.

Chapter 8:

Community Building and Support

In a world where survival can often feel like a solitary struggle, community becomes one of our most powerful tools. The idea of "going it alone" may seem appealing to some, but the reality of long-term survival often requires the collective efforts of a group.

This chapter will explore how to foster a robust and supportive community in times of crisis, from identifying reliable partners to establishing roles.

Identifying Trustworthy Allies

Finding trustworthy allies is one of the most critical steps in this process. Identifying people who share similar values, possess useful skills, and are committed to mutual survival is essential. However, trust must be built carefully and deliberately, as the stakes in this environment are high, and poor judgment can lead to disastrous consequences.

The first element in identifying trustworthy allies is observing behaviors under stress. Crisis reveals character. People who remain calm, rational, and collaborative in difficult situations will likely be more reliable than those who panic, withdraw, or become aggressive. Know that actions speak louder than words in these moments. Someone can claim to be trustworthy, but if they hoard supplies, take unnecessary risks, or refuse to contribute to group efforts, their behavior will undermine any words of reassurance.

Another factor is skill-sharing. A diverse group of people with a wide range of skills is far more effective than a group in which everyone has the same abilities. Allies with complementary skills, like medical knowledge, mechanics, hunting, or shelter-building, can create a more self-sufficient community. For example, if you have first-aid experience, you can pair with someone skilled in hunting to ensure people are fed and to treat wounds and illnesses that may arise. Trust often grows when people recognize they can rely on each other's strengths.

Finally, establishing trust requires open communication. Even in a survival situation, being transparent about concerns, plans, and goals helps avoid misunderstandings. Open communication builds confidence. When everyone feels heard and valued, trust naturally deepens. Taking time to talk, share experiences, and honestly discuss expectations can lay the groundwork for a cohesive and supportive group dynamic.

Creating Shared Resources

Once you've gathered a group of reliable people, the next step is to pool resources for the community's collective well-being. The key to survival isn't just individual stockpiling; it's about creating a system in which everyone contributes and benefits from shared supplies. The creation of shared resources helps ensure no one person is left without while also fostering a sense of communal responsibility.

Shared resources can include food, water, tools, and knowledge. For example, one person may contribute extra fishing equipment, while another may have seeds for a garden. Together, these resources can form the basis of a sustainable food supply. Similarly, those with medical supplies can create a shared medical kit accessible to everyone in the event of an injury or illness. The goal is to create a system where everyone can access essential needs, even if their personal resources are depleted.

Your next goal is to establish a common storage area where supplies are kept safe and organized. It can be helpful to designate a secure location within your shelter where food, tools, and other critical resources are stored. Inventorying and managing supplies collectively guarantees everyone knows what's available, reducing waste and preventing people from unknowingly hoarding or overusing shared items.

However, resource sharing extends beyond physical items. Knowledge is one of the most valuable shared resources. Information about edible plants, navigation techniques, or first-aid skills strengthens the group. This way, knowledge isn't siloed but distributed, ensuring that others can take over essential tasks if someone is incapacitated.

Consider creating a system of shared resources that fosters a sense of community and interdependence. When people know they can rely on others and that they, in turn, will be supported, they become more open to contributing, trust grows, and the group functions cohesively.

Establishing Roles and Responsibilities

In a survival setting, clearly defined roles and responsibilities are of paramount value as they can maintain order and ensure that all necessary tasks are completed. Without this structure, confusion can arise, and important jobs may be overlooked, threatening the group's overall well-being. By designating specific tasks for each group member, you divide labor fairly so everyone can focus on the skills they excel in, enhancing the group's efficiency.

Assigning roles also requires an honest assessment of each person's strengths and limitations. For instance, someone with strong organizational skills will be well-suited to manage resources and track inventory, ensuring that nothing is wasted. Others might take on roles like hunting, gathering, or firewood collection. Likewise, if someone has experience with basic construction, they will be responsible for building and maintaining shelters. It's not just about physical tasks; someone who excels at maintaining group morale or resolving conflicts can play a key role in keeping the social structure intact.

Flexibility is equally important in establishing roles. Emergencies and unforeseen circumstances will arise, and people may need to step outside their assigned tasks to help in other areas. For example, a person responsible for hunting may fall ill, and others must temporarily fill that role. So, look and plan for all the group members to be cross-trained in basic skills, like food preparation, first aid, or fire-making, as it will prevent the group from collapsing if the main members cannot fulfill their duties.

It's also important to rotate certain responsibilities to prevent burnout and resentment. Some tasks, such as guarding the perimeter or maintaining the fire at night, can be exhausting or monotonous. By rotating these responsibilities, everyone shares the workload, and no one person feels overburdened by an unpleasant or tiring task.

Ultimately, when roles and responsibilities are clear, it reduces confusion, fosters teamwork, and creates accountability within the group. Everyone knows what is expected of them, which leads to greater productivity and a sense of ownership over the group's survival.

Communication Strategies in Emergencies

In a survival situation, communication comes at the top for maintaining cohesion and responding effectively to threats or challenges. Clear and efficient communication can prevent misunderstandings, alert the group to danger, and coordinate actions during an emergency. Setting a solid communication strategy helps every member stay informed, engaged, and able to act when needed.

One of the first steps in creating an effective communication strategy is designating clear signals for different types of emergencies. For example, a specific whistle or hand signal can be used to indicate that danger is near, such as an approaching threat or predator. These signals should be simple, easy to understand, and consistent across the group. It's also important to rehearse these signals regularly to ensure everyone knows how to respond quickly and appropriately.

Communication also comes in handy in decision-making. During a crisis, swift, collective decisions are necessary to ensure the safety of the group. Designating a straightforward decision-making process, whether it's based on consensus or leadership, helps avoid confusion. For instance, if there is a fire or a sudden flood, having one or two designated leaders make the final call can streamline the response and prevent arguments or delays in action.

Maintaining communication over longer distances may also be necessary, especially if group members are out foraging or scouting. Simple tools, like walkie-talkies, flares, or reflective signals, can be used to relay important information across greater distances. In situations in which these tools are unavailable, creating predetermined check-in times or routes can help everyone stay updated and safe. For example, foraging parties can be required to return by sunset or at regular intervals to update the group on their progress or any dangers they encounter.

Beyond emergency signals, regular communication about the group's status, needs, and concerns is also a must-have for long-term survival. Holding daily meetings or check-ins during which people can discuss resource management, plans for the day, or any emerging problems will help a lot. It will also ensure no one is left out of critical decisions. These meetings foster transparency and offer a platform for discussing disagreements or concerns in a structured way, preventing minor issues from escalating into more significant conflicts.

The importance of clear, calm communication cannot be overstated in times of crisis. Panic and confusion can lead to dangerous mistakes, while organized communication ensures everyone knows their role and understands the situation. Building strong communication strategies is vital for navigating the everyday challenges and emergencies that will inevitably arise in a gridless world.

Chapter 9:

Adapting to Environmental Challenges

When faced with the challenge of surviving without modern infrastructure, adapting to the natural environment becomes a matter of life and death. Understanding local ecosystems may come at the end, but it helps in survival. This knowledge can provide essential information on where to find food, water, and shelter and how to avoid dangers like predators or poisonous plants.

This chapter dives into how to harness nature's resources sustainably while predicting weather changes and dealing with seasonal shifts.

Understanding Local Ecosystems

Different ecosystems require different survival strategies. For example, in a forested environment, you can find abundant wood for building shelter and foraging for edible plants and mushrooms. However, such environments may also pose risks, such as poisonous plants or dangerous animals. It's essential to familiarize yourself with the specific flora and fauna of the area you find yourself in. This means learning to identify which plants are edible, which animals are native, and how the ecosystem changes with the seasons.

In a desert ecosystem, the focus will shift dramatically. Water has become the most precious resource; understanding where to find it, through natural springs, cacti, or other sources, is mandatory. Meanwhile, shelter takes on a different meaning, as the goal becomes protection from the sun during the day and retaining heat at night. In such a setting, tracking the movement of animals can also help indicate nearby water sources, as wildlife tends to congregate around these crucial areas.

Coastal environments offer yet another set of challenges and opportunities. While the sea can give away a wealth of resources, such as fish and shellfish, it also brings risks in the form of unpredictable tides, storms, and dangerous marine life. Knowledge of tidal patterns and understanding safe foraging times can make a big difference in coastal survival.

Simply put, it's about knowing what to take, how much to take, and how to avoid depleting vital resources the ecosystem depends on. This approach is not only about survival; it's about sustainably coexisting with nature.

Sustainable Resource Management

During tough situations, it becomes easier to focus on immediate needs and overlook the importance of long-term planning. However, sustainable resource management must not be neglected to ensure the ecosystem continues to provide what you need. Taking too much from a single resource, be it food, water, or firewood, can lead to depletion and make survival even more difficult in the future.

Start by adopting the principle of **taking only what you need**. This means harvesting plants in small quantities or catching only enough fish to feed your group for the day rather than overfishing and jeopardizing the population for the future. It's tempting to stockpile when you come across an abundant resource, but overharvesting can disrupt local ecosystems and make it harder to survive in the long run.

Consider **water management** as well. If you're fortunate enough to find a freshwater source, like a stream or lake, don't assume it's unlimited. Drawing large quantities for irrigation or washing can affect the flow and quality of the water over time. Instead, use water conservatively, employ basic filtration techniques to ensure safe drinking water, and encourage the replenishment of natural sources.

In terms of firewood, the temptation to chop down whole trees for a lasting supply will seem like a quick fix, but it can have devastating consequences for the environment. A better approach is to gather fallen branches or dry wood that the ecosystem can naturally replace. In colder climates, you will need to plan ahead and gather enough firewood for winter, but again, this needs to be done thoughtfully, with an eye toward long-term sustainability.

If you're growing food or tending to a survival garden, it's important to remember the principle of crop rotation, which prevents soil exhaustion and ensures your land remains fertile. You'll also want to plan for ways to collect seeds and preserve soil health through composting and mulching. It will ensure the ecosystem continues support- ing your food production efforts.

Managing resources sustainably ensures your survival and the survival of the ecosystem that supports you. This bal- ance is necessary, particularly when you're relying on the natural world to provide for all your needs.

Weather Prediction Techniques

One of the most significant challenges in a survival situation is dealing with the unpredictability of weather. Fortunately, there are techniques you can learn to anticipate weather changes, which can give you the edge in staying safe and prepared. Modern technology, like weather apps and forecasts, won't be available, so you must rely on natu- ral signs and observations to predict weather patterns.

Start by paying attention to the sky. Cloud formations can give you helpful information. For example, cumulus clouds that grow quickly in the afternoon can indicate thunder- storms later in the day. Cirrus clouds—thin, wispy clouds high in the sky—often signal a storm front is approaching, typically within twenty-four hours. Observing the color of the sky can also offer clues. A red sky at sunrise often means rain is on the way, while a red sky at sunset suggests good weather will follow.

Animals are another excellent source of weather predic- tion. Before a storm, birds often fly lower to the ground, and animals may become unusually active. Insects, like ants and bees, often retreat to their nests before heavy rain or storms. Watching wildlife closely can give you early signs of changing weather.

Changes in wind direction and strength also offer vital insights. A sudden shift in wind direction or a dramatic increase in wind speed can indicate a storm front is approaching. If you're near a body of water, keep an eye on the waves (look for larger, rougher waves), as they can be a sign that a storm is brewing.

Humidity and temperature changes are worth monitoring as well. A drop in temperature, especially in combination with a rise in humidity, can signal rain or snow. You can measure these changes using simple tools, like a homemade barometer, or even just by paying attention to how the air feels on your skin.

By learning these techniques, you can avoid being caught unprepared by sudden weather changes and take the necessary steps to protect yourself and your shelter.

Dealing with Seasonal Changes

Surviving through different seasons also needs careful planning and adaptation. Each season presents unique challenges, from the blistering heat of summer to the freezing cold of winter, and preparing for these changes is essential for long-term survival.

In summer, the primary concerns are staying hydrated and protecting yourself from the sun. High temperatures can lead to dehydration, heat exhaustion, and sunburn, so it's important to seek shade during the hottest parts of the day and ensure you have a reliable water source. Wearing light, loose-fitting clothing that covers your skin can help protect you from the sun's rays while allowing your body to stay cool. Additionally, finding ways to store and preserve water during the summer months will ensure you have enough as temperatures rise and sources dry up.

Fall is a transitional season and an ideal time to prepare for the harshness of winter. In many ecosystems, fall offers an abundance of food as plants ripen and animals prepare for the colder months. It's a great time to focus on gathering and preserving food through methods like drying, canning, or smoking. This season also presents an opportunity to collect firewood, fortify shelters, and repair any equipment before winter sets in.

Winter, on the other hand, is one of the most difficult times to survive. Cold temperatures, limited food sources, and harsh weather conditions mean you must rely on stored supplies and ensure your shelter is well-insulated. Hypothermia and frostbite are real dangers in cold climates, so keeping a fire going should be your priority. Extra layers of clothing, blankets, and other forms of insulation will help retain body heat. Besides this, it's crucial to ration supplies and avoid overexertion, as food and energy will be limited during this time.

Spring brings its own set of challenges, including unpredictable weather and the need to rebuild supplies after a long winter. Melting snow can cause flooding, and the shift in temperatures can bring heavy rains and storms. However, spring is also a time of renewal, offering the chance to plant crops, gather fresh food, and prepare for the next seasonal cycle. As animals become more active, hunting and fishing opportunities increase, and the growing availability of fresh plants means you can diversify your diet.

Adapting to these seasonal changes is key to long-term survival. By planning and adjusting your strategies according to the time of year, you can increase your chances of thriving no matter what the environment throws your way.

Chapter 10:

Thriving Beyond Survival

Survival is about more than just scraping by; it's about creating a life worth living even in the harshest circumstances. Once you've met your basic needs (food, water, shelter, and security), it's time to think about how you can do more than survive. Thriving in a gridless world means finding ways to balance survival with comfort, build new traditions, pass on knowledge to future generations, and plan for reintegrating with modern society—if and when that time comes.

Balancing Survival with Comfort

When you first find yourself in a survival situation, comfort may seem like a luxury you can't afford. But as time passes, balancing survival with comfort becomes vital for maintaining your mental and physical health. Comfort doesn't just mean physical ease; it also means emotional stability, a sense of security, and even moments of joy. These elements contribute to long-term resilience.

One of the simplest ways to create comfort is through minor improvements in your living space. If you've constructed a basic shelter, think about ways to make it more livable. Adding a layer of insulation can keep you warm and make the shelter more comfortable to sleep in. Building a proper bedframe to elevate yourself off the ground can drastically improve sleep quality and, in turn, your mood and energy levels. Adding small touches in the form of woven mats, blankets, or even simple decorations made from natural materials can make your space feel like more of a home, even in the wild.

Comfort also comes in the form of routine. Having a daily schedule, even if it's built around survival tasks, like gathering food or tending to a garden, can deliver a sense of normalcy. Over time, this routine will become comforting in itself. It helps combat the chaos and unpredictability that often accompanies survival scenarios.

Finally, think about what brings you joy and find ways to incorporate it into your life. Whether it's reading a book, singing, or finding creative outlets like carving or painting, these small moments of pleasure can make a huge difference in how you feel about your situation. Thriving beyond survival means remembering that life can still be enjoyable, even in the hardest of times.

Creating Cultural Traditions

In a survival scenario, especially one that spans an extended period, fostering a sense of community and belonging is vital. One way to do this is by creating cultural traditions that give meaning to your new way of life. Traditions help mark the passage of time, create shared memories, and build a sense of continuity with the past while adapting to the present.

You can start by establishing rituals around meals or seasonal changes. For example, you can celebrate the first harvest of the season with a communal meal in which everyone contributes something they've gathered or grown. This doesn't just provide nourishment; it strengthens the bonds between people and reinforces the importance of working together.

Another form of tradition could come through storytelling. Passing down stories about your past experiences, your ancestors, or the challenges you've faced since living off the grid can build a shared narrative that binds the group together. These stories don't have to be dramatic or epic; they can be as simple as recounting a challenging hunting trip or a joyful moment of discovery in the wild. Over time, these stories become your group's myths and legends, helping foster a sense of identity and purpose.

Celebrating milestones is another way to create tradition. Birthdays, anniversaries, or even the changing of seasons can all be marked with small ceremonies or gatherings. These moments offer a reprieve from the daily grind of survival and give everyone something to look forward to, boosting morale and creating lasting memories.

Educational Opportunities for Future Generations

If you're in a survival situation long enough, children or future generations will inevitably become a part of the community. Their survival depends not only on having enough food and shelter but also on the education and knowledge passed down to them. Teaching them practical survival skills is, of course, need of the hour, but it's also important to provide them with broader educational opportunities that teach them curiosity, creativity, and critical thinking.

Begin with the basics: teaching children how to forage, hunt, or fish safely and sustainably. Show them how to identify edible plants and use natural resources without depleting them. Let them help with tasks like building shelters, gathering wood, and filtering water. These skills will keep them alive and give them a sense of agency and independence.

However, education shouldn't stop at survival skills. Teach future generations about the world that existed before the grid went down, from history and literature to science and art. Use any materials you have, books, oral history, or even your own knowledge to keep their minds engaged. If there's no access to traditional school supplies, improvisation is key. You can teach math through real-world scenarios, like calculating how much food you need for the winter or how far you can travel in a day. You can teach biology by studying local plants and animals or astronomy by mapping the stars.

The goal is to create well-rounded people who are not just focused on immediate survival. Instead, you're helping them think critically about the future and their place in it. These educational opportunities provide children with a sense of purpose and connection to a world that may one day recover from its current state.

Planning for Reintegration with Modern Society

While living off the grid might seem like a permanent reality, the possibility of reintegration with modern society is always a consideration. Whether through rebuilding infrastructure or making contact with other groups, planning for the future involves thinking about how you and your community will navigate a return to the broader world.

The first step in planning for reintegration is keeping skills and knowledge up-to-date. Just because modern society may be in shambles doesn't mean it's gone forever. Maintaining certain skills, like reading, writing, and mathematics, ensures you can adapt to a changing world if and when modern systems start to function again. Additionally, continuing to teach and learn about technology, even if it's no longer in use, can be beneficial. You never know when you might regain access to tools like radios, solar panels, or vehicles, so a basic understanding of how they work will be invaluable in the future.

Another aspect of planning for reintegration involves keeping communication channels open. This means setting up a makeshift radio station to try and contact other survivors or keeping records of your experiences that might one day be shared with others. If you're part of a larger group, it's essential to consider how you'll reintegrate with other communities. What resources or skills do you have that might be valuable to others? What cultural practices have you developed that you'd want to preserve? Answering these questions now will make the transition back to modern life smoother if it ever happens.

It's also important to remain adaptable. Reintegration might not happen all at once, or it might come with unexpected challenges. Staying flexible and open-minded about how society might evolve is key to thriving in a postapocalyptic world. Perhaps modern society will rebuild in a more sustainable or community-oriented way, and you'll need to adjust your expectations and practices accordingly.

Finally, think about the psychological and emotional challenges that come with reintegration. After spending so much time in survival mode, adjusting to a more stable, less isolated life will be difficult. Preparing yourself and your group for these emotional shifts will help ensure a smoother transition when the time comes. Discussing what reintegration might look like, what challenges it could bring, and how you might handle those changes as a community can help mitigate the stress of returning to a world that's different from the one you left behind.

Conclusion

As we reach the end of *Essential Survival Projects for Off-Grid Living: The Ultimate No-Grid Preparedness Kit for Busy People. Master Your Self-Sufficiency in Moments of Crisis*, it's important to reflect on the core strategies and skills we've explored and the crucial role they play in surviving and thriving in a gridless future. Our journey together through these pages has been about more than simply learning how to endure hardships. It's about equipping yourself with the knowledge, confidence, and resilience needed to turn survival into a way of life, even when modern conveniences have crumbled away.

Throughout this book, we've explored the fundamentals of survival in a world without the comforts of electricity, clean water at the turn of a tap, and easy access to food and shelter. Each chapter has focused on essential skills like securing water, producing and preserving food, building effective shelters, ensuring self-defense, and fostering mental resilience. Beyond that, we've also talked about building supportive communities, passing on knowledge to future generations, and even planning for the possibility of reintegrating into modern society one day.

These aren't just survival tips; they are strategies designed to help you thrive in a world that demands adaptability, resourcefulness, and mental strength. Let's revisit some key takeaways from each of these chapters to cement their importance and highlight how they can be practically applied to your life in a post-grid world:

Securing clean, safe water sources is perhaps the most critical survival skill. We've discussed finding natural water sources, like rivers, lakes, and rainwater, and purification techniques, such as boiling and filtration. Each method has its place depending on the circumstances, and knowing how to implement them means you can consistently provide yourself and others with life-sustaining hydration.

Food production and preservation were also covered in detail. Starting a sustainable garden provides fresh produce and instills a sense of control over your environment. Whether you're foraging for wild edibles or learning the basics of hunting and fishing, knowing where your next meal is coming from brings peace of mind. Preservation techniques like drying, canning, and fermenting ensure your hard-earned food lasts through harsh seasons when resources may be scarce.

Building a reliable, comfortable shelter is another survival element. We explored the importance of selecting strategic locations that protect you from environmental hazards while also considering insulation and structural integrity. Whether you're crafting a basic lean-to or a more sophisticated structure, the principles of shelter-building ensure your safety and comfort in unpredictable climates.

Alongside shelter, personal and community security is paramount. Crafting primitive weapons for defense and setting up perimeters can protect you from wildlife and other potential threats. This isn't about living in constant fear but being prepared and confident in your ability to defend yourself and your loved ones if necessary.

Identifying edible plants and foraging is a skill that empowers you to live more sustainably in a gridless future. By connecting with nature and understanding the food that surrounds you, you cultivate a deeper appreciation for the environment and the resources it offers. As you explore the wild for edible plants, remember to respect the land and practice responsible harvesting techniques. Whether you're adding wild greens to your dinner table or gathering berries for a sweet treat, the world of foraging is rich with opportunity and adventure. Embrace the journey, and let nature nourish you.

Survival isn't only physical; it's deeply psychological. Managing stress in crises, building a positive outlook, and maintaining mental resilience are just as crucial as securing food and water. We talked about the techniques for overcoming fear and establishing routines to create stability. In challenging times, mental strength often becomes your greatest asset. Finding moments of joy, establishing comforting rituals, and fostering a sense of normalcy can make even the most difficult situations bearable.

By understanding the principles of heat transfer and employing a combination of natural and manufactured materials, you can create a comfortable and safe shelter. Know that effective insulation protects against extreme weather and contributes to your overall well-being in uncertain conditions. With practice and creativity, you'll be well-equipped to insulate your shelter and thrive, no matter the environment you face.

Community plays a vital role in survival. Building a network of trustworthy allies, sharing resources, and establishing roles and responsibilities within the group are crucial to fostering cooperation. A strong community increases the chances of survival exponentially, as each member brings unique skills, knowledge, and strengths to the table. In times of crisis, shared effort and mutual support can turn an overwhelming challenge into something surmountable.

One of the most important lessons you can take from this book is that survival is an ongoing process. No matter how much you prepare, you'll always encounter new challenges, unexpected situations, and evolving threats. That's why continuous learning is essential. The world we've described is constantly changing, and your ability to adapt, learn, and grow will determine your success.

Whether it's learning new foraging techniques, improving your self-defense skills, or figuring out more efficient ways to produce and store food, there's always room for growth. The information in this book is a foundation, but the real strength lies in your willingness to keep building on it. Keep exploring, testing, and refining your skills. Seek out other sources of knowledge, and don't be afraid to experiment and innovate.

Survival isn't a static goal. It's a journey; the more you learn, the more equipped you'll be to handle whatever comes your way. Embrace the challenges as opportunities to grow stronger, smarter, and more resilient.

Living off the grid may seem daunting, but it's important to remember that hope is a powerful tool in your survival kit. Surviving and thriving in such a world doesn't have to mean living in isolation, hardship, or constant struggle. It can be a chance to rebuild in a way that reflects your values, priorities, and dreams.

Imagine creating a world where you and your community live sustainably, where the focus shifts from consumption to self-sufficiency, relationships are built on cooperation, and every day is filled with purpose. The skills you've learned don't just help you survive; they offer you a path to a richer and more intentional life.

There's hope in the idea that even in the most difficult circumstances, you have the ability to adapt, innovate, and overcome. There's hope in the community, in the bonds we form when we work together to face challenges. There's hope in knowing that as long as you continue learning and growing, you'll be able to handle whatever the future holds.

Ultimately, thriving in a gridless world isn't just about out-lasting hardship—it's about building a future in which you can live with dignity, comfort, and fulfillment. It's about re-connecting with the natural world, rebuilding communities, and passing on knowledge and skills to future generations.

As you close this book, I want to thank you for embarking on this journey with me. The skills and strategies you've learned here are powerful tools for surviving and thriving. Whether you're already preparing for a future without the modern conveniences we've become accustomed to or simply seeking to become more self-reliant in your every-day life, I hope this book has provided valuable insights.

Most importantly, know that this book is just the beginning of your journey into off-grid survival. We already have covered a broad range of essential topics that will serve as a starting point to help you think critically, adapt creatively, and understand survival isn't about following a one-size-fits-all approach.

This book is your call to implement what you've learned here to your unique circumstances. The absence of numerous illustrations is intentional; this book isn't meant to dictate exact methods but to inspire you to adapt to your environment with creativity and resourcefulness. If you'd prefer an audiobook version of this book, the lack of illustrations ensures nothing gets lost in translation. I hope you'll share your feedback with me as you put these ideas into practice.

I encourage you to leave a review of this book. Your feedback is invaluable and helps guide others who are on the same journey toward self-sufficiency. Let me know what resonated with you, what strategies you found most helpful, and how you plan to implement these ideas in your life. Your thoughts will inspire others to take control of their futures and equip themselves with the skills needed to thrive, no matter what challenges come their way.

Also, I would like to request that you please leave suggestions on what topics you would like me to cover and what topics you want me to cover in more detail in subsequent books. Your suggestions will help me shape future content, and I genuinely look forward to reading every comment.

Thank you again for reading *Essential Survival Projects for Off-Grid Living*!

References

Ali, Ahtisham, Shuai Wei, Adnan Ali, Imran Khan, Qinxiu Sun, Qiuyu Xia, Zefu Wang, Zongyuan Han, Yan Liu, and Shuncheng Liu, "Research progress on nutritional value, preservation and processing of fish—A review." *Foods, 11*(22), 3669, November 16, 2022, https://doi.org/10.3390/foods11223669.

Barrell, Amanda, "How to Perform CPR: Guidelines, Procedure, and Ratio," *Medical News Today,* May 22, 2023, https://www.medicalnewstoday.com/articles/324712.

Bente, Dennis, "Leptospirosis: An Outbreak Following Hurricane Maria in Puerto Rico," *LinkedIn,* January 24, 2024, https://www.linkedin.com/pulse/leptospirosis-outbreak-following-hurricane-maria-rico-bente-dvm-phd-dfayc.

Buchele, Mose, "Two Years Later, the 2021 Blackout Still Shapes What It Means to Live in Texas," *NPR,* February 17, 2023, https://www.npr.org/2023/02/17/1157847354/texas-blackout-2021-still-haunts.

Cherry, Kendra, "Maslow's hierarchy of needs," *VeryWellMind,* April 2, 2024, https://www.verywellmind.com/what-is-maslows-hierarchy-of-needs-4136760.

Editors of EarthSky, "Use the Big Dipper to Find the Little Dipper", *EarthSky*, April 14,2024, https://earthsky.org/tonight/use-big-dipper-to-find-polaris-and-little-dipper/.

Filippone, Peggy Trowbridge, "Edible Mushroom Varieties," *The Spruce Eats*, February 16, 2023, https://www.thespruceeats.com/edible-mushroom-varieties-1807698.

Guendelman, Simon, Sebastian Medeiros, and Hagen Rampes, "Mindfulness and Emotion Regulation: Insights from Neurobiological, Psychological, and Clinical Studies," *Frontiers in Psychology*, *8*(8), March 5, 2017, https://doi.org/10.3389/fpsyg.2017.00220.

Gunnars, Kris, "How Much Water Should You Drink Per Day?," *Healthline*, June 5, 2023, https://www.healthline.com/nutrition/how-much-water-should-you-drink-per-day.

History.com Editors, "Blackout Hits Northeast United States," *This Day in History*, *History*, August 21, 2018, https://www.history.com/this-day-in-history/blackout-hits-northeast-united-states.

Hoyt, Alia, "How Igloos Work," *HowStuffWorks*, January 17, 2008, https://people.howstuffworks.com/igloo.htm.

Maček, Ivana, "Transmission and Transformation: Memories of the Siege of Sarajevo," *Civilians under Siege from Sarajevo to Troy*, 15–35, December 14, 2017, https://doi.org/10.1057/978-1-137-58532-5_2.

MasterClass, "19 Edible Wild Plants That Are Safe to Forage," *MasterClass*, May 10, 2022, https://www.masterclass.com/articles/edible-wild-plants.

Palin, Philip J., "The Role of Groceries in Response to Catastrophes," *CNA*, January 2017, https://www.cna.org/archive/CNA_Files/pdf/final-the-role-of-groceries-in-response-to-catastrophe.pdf.

Serena, Katie, "How Aron Ralston's Harrowing Survival Story Inspired '127 Hours,'" *All That's Interesting*, October 29, 2023, https://allthatsinteresting.com/aron-ralston.